Love

Love

The Foundation of Christian Thought and Wisdom

RODNEY WEEMS

RESOURCE *Publications* · Eugene, Oregon

LOVE
The Foundation of Christian Thought and Wisdom

Copyright © 2022 Rodney A. Weems. All rights reserved. Except for brief quotations in critical publications or reviews, no part of this book may be reproduced in any manner without prior written permission from the publisher. Write: Permissions, Wipf and Stock Publishers, 199 W. 8th Ave., Suite 3, Eugene, OR 97401.

Resource Publications
An Imprint of Wipf and Stock Publishers
199 W. 8th Ave., Suite 3
Eugene, OR 97401

www.wipfandstock.com

PAPERBACK ISBN: 978-1-6667-3209-2
HARDCOVER ISBN: 978-1-6667-2538-4
EBOOK ISBN: 978-1-6667-2539-1

VERSION NUMBER 012822

Unless otherwise noted Scripture quotations are from The Catholic Edition of the Revised Standard Version of the Bible, copyright © 1965, 1966 by the National Council of the Churches of Christ in the United States of America. Used by permission. All rights reserved worldwide.

Scripture quotations marked (NIV) are taken from the Holy Bible, New International Version®, NIV®. Copyright © 1973, 1978, 1984, 2011 by Biblica, Inc.™ Used by permission of Zondervan. All rights reserved worldwide. www.zondervan.com The "NIV" and "New International Version" are trademarks registered in the United States Patent and Trademark Office by Biblica, Inc.™

Scripture quotations marked (AMP) are taken from the Amplified® Bible, Copyright © 2015 by The Lockman Foundation. Used by permission. www.lockman.org

This book is dedicated to Ethan and Eric—in the hope that all that is best in them and the world in which they live will come to fruition.

"Give us, O God, the gift of human charity. Lead us to know that bad as human nature is and black as our passion may be, that most men are always a little better than the worst, always more decent than our rash judgment tries to paint. Give us the humility to realize that few of us put in their places—with their hurts and hindrances and their vision of right—few of us would do better than they, and many would do far worse. Perhaps God meant just this when He said: *Blessed* are the meek. Amen."

—W. E. B. Du Bois

Contents

List of illustrations | ix
Acknowledgements | xi

Introduction | 1

The Problem | 3

The Conversation Where Opposites Agreed | 7

Epiphany and Transformation | 17

Reformation | 23

Rome Versus Corinth | 31

Faith, Hope, but Especially Love | 40

Faith, Hope, but Especially Love, Paraphrased | 50

The Tenets of Wise-Love | 52

Love and the Ten Commandments | 54

What Is Lost When Grace Is Lost | 60

Maturity through Grace and Love | 64

Evidence of the Protective Wisdom Love Provides | 73

Wise-Love Reprised | 78

Bibliography | 85

List of Illustrations

Figure 12-1 | 64
Figure 12-2 | 68

Acknowledgements

THERE ARE TIMES IT is hard to say thank you because the words fall so short of the gratitude one really feels. But maybe, in those cases, that is the point—to be discomforted with the humbling realization of how indebted we are to the grace of others. In somewhat the reverse order that they have entered my life, I would like to thank the following people.

First, as pertains to my fellow congregants at The Cathedral of the Nativity, Bethlehem, Pennsylvania: People from both sides of the political spectrum who are willing to discuss honestly and civilly the most challenging issues of the day seem to have become an endangered species. But they are alive and well at Nativity, and I am thankful for them—and for the careful and constant love of Dean Pompa who, in the name of Jesus Christ, has inspired us all to try and be more loving versions of ourselves.

Thank you also to Gregg Buczkowski who, over numerous phone calls, helped me finish growing the many conversational seeds that were sown at Nativity. If arriving at some closer approximation of wisdom or truth is like approaching a limit from both sides, Gregg is perhaps the only person in the world I could thank by saying how much I appreciate that he is the positive epsilon-delta to my negative.

In terms of the people who helped me persevere over the years that it took these ideas to come to life, I owe a tremendous debt of gratitude to my good friend Dr. Susanne "Zan" Struebing. Without her gentle insistence that I put my thoughts about life and

Acknowledgements

faith on paper, without her consistent willingness to read draft after chapter draft, and without her thoughtfulness in emailing me the conference flier that led me to Wipf and Stock, this book would likely not exist.

In a similar vein, thank you also to Dr. Sara Koenig, Professor of Theology at Seattle Pacific University. Sara has a knack for asking one or two questions about a manuscript that cut so precisely to the core of an issue that it often takes me a few months to see the deep implications resident in her questions. Everything I pass by Sara is better and kinder as a result of her efforts. To others who read, edited, and commented on various iterations of *Love*, to Pam Bowman, Gordon Tucker, Catherine Ambos, Valari Westeren, and to Wipf and Stock Publishers, thank you as well.

I am daily grateful to my endlessly clever mom and to Ms. Jacolyn Robbie, my fourth-grade teacher. I cannot imagine where I would be without their hours of working with me until I had tamed my dyslexia. Regarding my mom in particular, her insistence that we strive to make the best use we can of the gifts God gave us, as well as her continuous example (now eighty-eight years in the making) of what it means to live a life of peace-making service, stand silently behind many of the thoughts in this book.

Finally, I am humbled by my wife Kathleen's patience with my metronomic penchant for waking her up at five in the morning to talk ideas. How could I be anything other than thankful for her kindness in putting up with the quarks of a sometimes writer? I had my first inkling of wanting to marry her shortly after I ran out of gas on our third date and she kissed me rather than yelling. I would marry her again if time worked that way. To all of these wonderful people, I offer my deepest thanks.

Introduction

IN 2002 I VISITED Maine to see Gregg, my college roommate, and his young family. At the Naval Academy, Gregg and I made strange bedfellows: he was white, I was black; he was Catholic, I was Protestant; he was a Republican, I was a Democrat; he questioned climate change, I absolutely believed it was real. We were friends, not because of our similarities, but rather in spite of our differences. Except on one point: we both had just enough of the intellectual and theological rebel in us that we clicked. At the conclusion of that weekend visit, he gave me a Catholic Bible with a note and a finishing inscription that read, *P.S. Enjoy the "uncut" version ;)*

Over the years, long stretches of time passed before we saw each other again. When we were able to clear our calendars, our time together was always good. It was also predictable that by the end of whatever time we had, we never came to agree on much, except that society was becoming less and less what we thought it should be. That was the story of our friendship until I called him in May 2020. That is when I heard a string of yesses coming from the other end of the phone that startled me. There was some pushback on a few points, but we pretty much came to total agreement in the end.

This little book is about what we came to agreement on. It is about the fact that after I called him up a few weeks later to talk about the realization our conversation had brought me to, I also noticed that the Bible I was reading at that point was the one Gregg had given me eighteen years earlier. I cannot help but believe there

INTRODUCTION

was something divinely inspired in that—in two people, from opposite sides of almost every social fence, talking to each other as friends and coming to a common understanding about what God had been trying to say to us over all those years. The message underlying that commonality is for pastors, priests, and other members of the clergy. If you belong to a church where you have never been tempted to call the congregation the audience, then it is also for you.

In the pages that follow, I intend to write as Paul wrote, as if in a letter between friends, "not in lofty words or wisdom" dripping with clever logic. I will say this much of my own accord: over the days that this message has unfolded, I have been surprised by tears on more than one occasion. Not something that a military guy like me will easily admit to. My hope is that these chapters will likewise move you—beyond faith, beyond tears, and into the love of God to which these words are meant most directly to speak.

The Problem

I HAD JUST FINISHED reading the Scriptures before the congregation. Now, it was time to pass the peace. As I reached out my hand to greet the Caucasian woman next to me, she likewise reached out her hand. But before hers touched mine, she jerked it back with an unmistakable look of disgust, the reality of my skin color having finally registered with her. As if choreographed in advance, she pirouetted and began shaking hands in the opposite direction without a word. Standing there, I wondered if she felt any contradiction between her actions and those advocated by the Holy Bible passages I had just read. And I wondered, yet again, why a place that is supposed to embody love is responsible for so much hate.

These were not emotional questions. They were logical questions, theological questions. I wanted her to explain what biblical justification she could muster for treating me so shabbily. I wanted chapter and verse laid out with syllogistic precision. But I knew that if I wanted an answer of this type, I was going to have to search the Scriptures for myself.

With this aim—to understand the biblical logic embraced by so many people—I began to ponder why our thoughts on a multitude of issues were often diametrically opposed. I wanted to know why our views on abortion, imprisonment, women's rights, and a host of other matters seemed as if they were formed while reading two different Bibles.

No matter how I tried to reconcile our differences, the end was frequently the same: I was wrong from their perspective, and they were unquestionably right. Yet, I could not help but think their approach lacked humility, especially in light of 1 Corinthians 8:1–3, which says, "'All of us possess knowledge.' 'Knowledge' puffs up, but love builds up. If anyone imagines that he knows something [for certain], he does not yet know as he ought to know. But if one loves God, one is known by him."

These verses echo Socrates and his assertion that he was wisest among the Greeks of his time because he alone knew that he knew nothing. He was willing to fully listen to other people because he was willing to suspend his own sense of certainty—an essential stance in a complex world that we can accurately understand only from the perspective of multiple, overlapping co-narratives. This was my starting point in trying to understand alternative interpretations of the Bible by which so much hate was and is justified.

Because modern biblical interpretations are unavoidably colored by the preconceived logic of our time, there is no current topic neutral enough to use as a basis for an unbiased examination of these different interpretations. If transported back in time, however, most modern Christians would argue with full conviction that lynching is morally wrong. They would stand aghast as their ancestors—dressed in their Sunday best, perhaps having just sung "Amazing Grace"—exit the church, walk to a nearby vale, open up their picnic baskets, sit smiling beside their children, and wait . . . to enjoy a lynching.

There, in that not-so-distant time and place, many believers would find themselves in exactly the position I find myself in today. They would stand face-to-face with Christian brothers and sisters of old who would fully and forcefully argue that modern Christians are wrong. Those ancestors would justify by chapter and verse "how niggers can be lynched high and long" with no remorse. They would argue against our more modern biblical interpretations with the same righteous certainty that many modern fundamentalists hold their own stances today.

Try to understand the logic of their position. See if you can mount an argument using only Scripture to justify the enslavement, torture, hanging, and immolation of another human being.

The Problem

Most people will have trouble finding such support. But blacks who came of age in twentieth-century America will have no trouble doing so. During that time, knowledge of such arguments was part and parcel of every black person's education.

Tenable arguments supporting the enslavement of blacks and whites are easy to find in the Bible. It is harder to find biblical support for the tragic abuses that occurred once black slaves were no longer protected by being considered property. After the law abolished slavery, many Christians were nonetheless among the most vociferous in their justification of lynching blacks. So why the continuation of such hatred from Bible-loving people?

When I first asked this question of fellow churchgoers one Sunday morning, most people had no answer to this inquiry. So, I explained about the descendants of Cain, who were supposedly cursed with a black mark (black skin in the southern telling), and about the sons of Hamm, who were cursed because their forefather saw Noah's nakedness. But since most of these old excuses have gone by the wayside, the best explanation hinged on a reading of Genesis that pointed out how Adam and Eve were given dominion over all the animals of the earth. If blacks were viewed as animals—or at least as dirty, uncivilized, and thus less than human—then the white Adams and Eves of the world could do with them what they wanted.

Yet even that explanation had a worm in the middle because in the Bible, people given dominion are usually given it so they can act as Peter, Jesus, and Ruth did—as caretakers, servants, and helpers. Therefore, the question remained, Why did so many people take Genesis, numerous other biblical passages, and ultimately their religion as a whole, to mean that the world was theirs? Why did such a worldview justify the stance that Germany, America, or other regions belonged to them and that they could treat other, *lesser* people in whatever way they pleased? How, I wanted to know, did such a sense of pride, superiority, and exceptionalism—along with the hatreds that often resulted—become so hard-baked into the Western spiritual tradition of so many people?

Today in America and throughout the world, it is as if we have received two different gospels. When I ask my father-in-law why he believes so differently than I do, when I ask him how he can be so sure that his interpretation of the Bible is right and my interpretation of the Bible is wrong, he replies with a different verse than I would pick. He quotes 1 Corinthians 2:14–16: "The unspiritual man does not receive the gifts of the Spirit of God, for they are folly to him, and he is not able to understand them because they are spiritually discerned. The spiritual man judges all things, but is himself to be judged by no one. 'For who has known the mind of the Lord so as to instruct him?' But we have the mind of Christ." My father-in-law says this as if to imply that he has the Spirit and, clearly, I do not. How can I refute that? How does anyone reply without falling into the same sense of pride and self-certainty that he seems to be exhibiting toward me?

Since I was twelve years old, whenever I felt that my understanding of a particular Scripture conflicted with my understanding of Christian love, it has been a sure guide that I was wrong either in my understanding of Scripture or in my understanding of love. But as a young Christian, I was never able to be 100 percent sure which it was. Even once I became more confident of my sense of what godly love demanded, my understanding remained so intuitive that the only defense I could give paralleled what my father-in-law had to say about the matter.

Being a mathematician, I wanted more. I wanted a reasonable certainty. I wanted something that would keep me from falling prey to false prophets, errant priests, and my own selfish desires. I wanted a scriptural basis for my understanding of the demands of Christian love that was every bit as clear as the hope we have in Christ. That was what I *stumbled* across a few weeks after I spoke with my friend.

The next chapter recounts the conversation between Gregg and me that led to my epiphany. It serves as a bridge to the chapters that follow it, chapters that introduce the epiphany itself—and the startling, all-encompassing scriptural centrality of what I have come to call *wise-love*

The Conversation Where Opposites Agreed

THE PIVOTAL CONVERSATION BETWEEN Gregg and myself began with me recounting that near the end of my first year at the Naval Academy, I received what I will call a pink slip. As midshipmen, we knew the officers were watching us. But most of us had no idea that our professors were also evaluating our fitness for military service. I became one of the few to realize that if instructors noticed a detrimental trait, they could submit a form that outlined the thinking behind their assessment. That explains how one day, I found a paper in my mailbox questioning my fitness for future naval service. One of my physics professors felt that I required too much information before I was willing to make a decision. He viewed that element of character as a negative indicator of success and said so on his form. Livid at what seemed an unwarranted threat to my future, I went to confront the man.

He knew why I was there the moment I entered his classroom. Skipping the pleasantries, I got straight to the point. I asked if he had been the one who submitted the form and, if so, how he felt qualified to make such a consequential assessment. After all, I pointed out without any sense of irony, he barely knew me. Our interactions had been limited to classroom questions and one social event beyond the classroom walls. There was not a single reply he could have given that I would have accepted as justification for his stance . . . except the one that came out of his mouth: "Because I recognize myself in you."

Caught by surprise, I had to entertain the truth of his answer, if for no other reason than that I, indeed, sensed the same truth about him. So I asked for more of an explanation. He obliged by saying, "In a tactical situation, like the one a submarine commander might encounter at sea, often an officer will lack the data required to make a fully informed decision. But he must act anyway. If he waits too long, he and his crew may die. You would have trouble in situations like that. Always wanting a bit more information before acting, you would doom yourself and your crew."

I had little to say after that. I thanked him, turned around, and left. But not without learning a lesson from the interaction. From that day forward, I began to ponder if it was possible to act reliably and ethically without having all the pieces of a situational puzzle. Was there a way, a repeatable method people could use, to be reasonably assured of acting beforehand in the same fashion they would also act if given 20/20 hindsight? That was probably the first time I solidly glimpsed what I would come to see as the distinction between wisdom and knowledge.

Knowledge is composed of people piling fact after fact, one atop another, as they seem to progress ever closer to *the truth*. But knowledge is also understanding that hovering in the background is the possibility that the next newly acquired fact could radically change their perspective on the whole. It is knowing there is something around the corner but also knowing that they are not going to be sure what it is, no matter how many facts they collect, until they are close enough to round the corner and look.

Wisdom, on the other hand, is foresight. It is the ability to render decisions in the absence of a complete fact set, decisions that nonetheless accord with the ones people would have made if they had already rounded the corner and could act in hindsight. As a practical matter, wisdom also entails the understanding that there is always more information resident in a situation than most people realize.

Seeing Character and Using
Its Universally Deep Patterns

Many years after this interaction with my professor, a neighbor asked if I would like to play a game of horseshoes. This was a guy who practiced daily in his own pit. So, when I said "yes" to his invite, I also accepted that I would likely lose. Within a few rounds, his 7–0 lead affirmed my estimate. Had I missed the lesson my professor inadvertently taught me at the academy, I would have resigned myself to defeat. Instead, the part of me that had come to understand that every situation offers us more information than we are aware of kicked into gear.

Focusing on my body's kinesthetics as I made the following toss, I realized that the action of throwing a horseshoe is almost the same as throwing a bowling ball. If I knew anything about bowling, I knew that good bowlers never aim at the pins. They always aim at the arrows that point the way to the pins. With that idea in hand, I quit focusing on the horseshoe stake and began aiming at an imaginary arrow I visualized in the air a few feet away. That was the round in which I scored my first point. A few points came in the next round, then a few more, until I eventually won.

But taking such an analogy-based approach to life's problems is difficult. In situations where we lack skill or knowledge, the surface realities of the situation misdirect us with an obvious set of distracting facts that are only modestly useful. All the while, more consequential streams of information lie hidden beneath the surface. They are present in the psychology of the situation, the science behind the situation, the historical precedents involved in the situation, the spiritual context of the situation, and so on. Wisdom never broadcasts itself exclusively on any single channel. Instead, wisdom resonates across the whole.

Just as middle-C sounds the same but different on a flute, piano, or oboe, the most profound wisdom and the most crucial life patterns are independent of name or surface identity. The flight of a basketball, a ballistic missile, and that man on the flying trapeze all have the same character by virtue of the parabolic path dictated by earth's gravitational pull. In biology, a green tree, a human lung, and the roots of a bush display similar characteristic shapes because all are performing some version of breathing—of exhaling waste and inhaling nutrients. The prevalence of such universal principles throughout life explains why horseshoes and bowling are interchangeable on many levels. It is also why prioritizing character—the deep, universal patterns inherent in all life—is useful in helping people find wise bearings in shifting and uncertain seas. Focusing on character rather than on labels or surface appearances is essential because things that seem least related externally are often twins internally.

Christian Character

Do people want to understand the God they purport to believe in or the character of the religion they have built around that belief? Then they should forget the name attached to what they believe and look at the internal patterns and principles embodied in the stances favored by their belief system.

Does a religion that believes crusades are best waged by brute force, guns, and violence truly have the same character as a religion that believes crusades should be waged by lives lived with such peaceable excellence that others are conquered by sheer force of example? Or does a religion that refuses to reckon with a pattern of tribal sins have the same character as a religion that believes life in Christ is about grace amid the shadow of acknowledged sin? What about a religion derived from a perspective that prizes the status of masters? Does that compare to a religion that seeks would-be servants and elevates the last over the first?

These examples differentiate between people who call themselves Christians but who are perfectly happy worshiping at the altar of Mammon, and others who also call themselves Christians but who try hard not to bow their heads there.

When I first submitted this manuscript for proofreading, the editor suggested that I use a word other than *Mammon* because she believed it would be unfamiliar to most people. We chose

The Conversation Where Opposites Agreed

money as the synonym because that is the translation used in most modern Bibles when seeking to clarify the text for today's readers. The replacement was ineffective. But I failed to understand why until I realized that Christ wanted us to perceive Mammon as a God—not merely a little-g god, but one who visits us with all the promises in hand that any counterfeit god worth his salt should guarantee.

The Amplified Bible summarizes Mammon by explaining It as "[money, possessions, fame, status, or whatever is valued more than the Lord]" (Matt. 6:24 (AMP)). A considerable portion of the first commandment is encapsulated in God's request not to bow to Mammon. Why? Because money is never just money, is it? It is all the things we believe money—as if it is some omnipotent god—can give us: control, security, power, social mobility, the illusion of love, the chimera of happiness . . . you name it; the God Mammon promises to supply it. In disguised tones, He promises to do so with a bottom-line regularity that the prayers of faithful worshipers often seem to lack.

From start to finish, Mammon strides through the Bible with abandon. He goes almost unnoticed except among the red-letter words where Christ calls him by his actual name. Yet there Mammon is at the side of the rich young ruler who would have gladly given away all his possessions and money, if only he did not fear that his access to power and status might also walk out the door after such an insult to his green God.

In a recent Sunday school class, my fifth graders realized that Mammon was also present when God compared the kingdom of heaven to the pearl of great price, the jewel that could be held only if a person was willing to give up everything to possess it. As they contemplated whether this included forfeiting their Nintendo Switches, iPhones, cars, and houses, Mammon made an honest plea for moderation.[1]

---

1. Sifting through all the giggles of that day, I find it interesting to remember that the answer most kids gave for what they would do hinged on their friends, who they assured me would always be there for them, almost like God's temples, like the places of refuge the Bible says we are all supposed to be for each other . . . and probably would be, if we weren't so stretched by time,

He was also on the shore when Christ came to ask Peter and Andrew if they would leave their work and go with him to be fishers of men. What Christian has not asked if he or she would likewise drop a job and follow Christ if he asked that same personal question today? Of course, many people suspect he never will, so they soon dismiss the question's implications.

But I recently realized that Christ is asking us some version of this same question almost daily in many of today's capitalist societies. Because most of my adult life has been spent as a teacher, I can speak only to how Christ and Mammon have come to me in the classroom. In that context, what is it when your boss tells you to pass a student who you know deserves an F, who you know needs another year of schooling that only that F will grant—but the boss wants him passed, and you, as a teacher, want to keep your job?

During COVID, many administrators asked teachers to pass 50 percent or more of kids who deserved to fail. School systems asked instructors to water down tests, to overlook hundred-percent absentees, to do all manner of deeds that no educator of good moral character would think of doing of their own accord. Will we come with Christ and do the right thing? Or stay by the shore and do the practical thing, the thing needed to ensure that we haul in a net gain of fish and money?

When Christ was tempted on high and Pilate washed his hands, when the heads of kings and queens rolled in Paris and the blood of Tsars flowed after that, Mick Jagger had it right as he sang, "Pleased to meet you / Hope you guessed my name / But what's puzzling you / Is the nature of my game."

Year after year, age after age, that is the question. Look closer to home, at the old South as well as the on-and-off complicity of the North. You will see two societies confronted with this same timeless question: Is earning money (an entire economic system's worth of money and security for the few) more or less important than the preservation of life and liberty for all? Is worshiping at the

---

money, and, one day, a significant other who might eventually say it is time for that freeloader to go.

altar of Mammon more or less wise than pledging allegiance to the dignity of human life and the love of all neighbors?

In service to protecting the Southern way of life, the full-throated way in which many Southern Christians chose to exploit both their land and the black slaves that worked that land is testament to their response. So, too, is the degree to which the North's financial and industrial growth was tethered to that wagon and how even some African-American slaveowners betrayed their own kind for a few pieces of silver. Though obscured, the ethical reality of these choices echoes even today.

Consider modern Appalachians—stereotypically Caucasian, but also African-American and a smattering of other races. They feel no great allegiance to either the North or the South. Yet with decrepit lungs ravaged by coal dust, these blue-mountain men profess love and loyalty to culture, heritage, and the almighty dollar. They stoically wake to the new day. With their last, aching breaths, they beg for the continuance of their way of life and the coal-earned dollars that will make it possible to pass that same painful, black-lunged birthright down to their children.

We toss the word *socio-economic* around so lightly these days that many people fail to realize the profound truth embodied by the compound: the economic choices we make to earn our money inextricably shape society and lives in that society. Some people live to work; others work to live. Some societies value economic gain more than life or the dignity of life. Other societies favor life over maximizing economic gain.

It is easy to skip over this aspect of the first commandment with hardly a thought. But this was the commandment the devil hoped Jesus would break when he gave our Savior the universal choice to pick between security, provision, and power or serving the God who always sides with life in opposition to the wretched social contracts often written in favor of the bottom line (see Matt. 4:1–11; Mark 1:12–13; Luke 4:1–13). It was the choice offered to the agrarian South, the industrial North, and a century-and-a-half's worth of coal miners. It is the choice offered even today, when the clear question in this time of virus and climate change is whether to favor our addiction to maximized, short-term job creation and profits over life or to prioritize life and the long-term survival of life on the planet over socio-economic creature comforts.

The Greatest Wisdom

Among the possible strands from which we can attempt to weave wisdom, some threads are significantly more important to the strength and character of the whole than others. Bottom-line considerations have their place in the weave. But the most important of all those strands is the knowledge and power of love.

People can debate whether the Bible is a book that is primarily about wisdom or mostly about love. Actually, it is about both. For love, when rightly defined, is its own kind of wisdom. Because Christianity is the religious tradition in which I was raised, I will use the Bible as my reference point in talking about love. But to my mind, the Bible, Torah, Koran, Bhagavad-Gita, and many other holy stories and texts are all meant to help people who have quietly come to realize that they often stumble around in the dark for lack of the information they need to make wise life decisions.

We raise children, feeling like we are making it up as we go, wishing we had a better instruction manual. We pick marriage partners, wondering at the altar if we have made the right choice in the face of fifty-percent failure rates. We vote for politicians without having had the time to read across the spectrum of options due to busy lives. We confront complex societal issues without a decent comprehension of basic science or mathematics. And although many Christians like to claim that the United States is a Christian nation, sixty-eight percent of Americans have failed to read all or even most of the Bible.[2]

Recognition of our ignorance throws us back onto the shores of this conversation's beginning, where we asked, "Is there a way to make wise decisions in the absence of sufficient knowledge and time?" Is there a way to avoid the ricochet of self-destructive,

---

2. Banks, "Bible Not Read Much," para. 9.

The Conversation Where Opposites Agreed

unintended consequences that often follow in the wake of less than fully informed decisions?

The Bible's answer to this question is that choosing Love and the God who authored that love is always the best choice and, therefore, the foundation of true wisdom. The pragmatic, hard-nosed, bottom-line type of "Christianity" that tries to pass itself off as wise often delivers on its promises in the short term. But in the end, worshiping at Mammon's altar leads only to ruin.

So, from among all the different types of love, what constitutes the dividing line between what is and is not wise-love? Gregg wanted to know because there are as many ways to go about in the world as a supposedly loving person as there are spoken languages. There is tough love, romantic love, filial love, helpless love, love given to people who deserve to be loved, love given to the undeserving, and a thousand other variations. Gregg wanted to know which of those many love patterns the Bible defines as wise-love, as the north star that will guide us through the valley of death and leave us fearing no evil. Without such love, our attempts to act beforehand as if with 20/20 hindsight will fail.

In answer to Gregg's question, I said I was not sure exactly how the Bible defined such love, but I did know one thing: "Wise-love is not wise that is not humble." Love is not wise-love that favors only those in the same tribe as one's self while excluding others in the belief that they are lesser—less cultured, less human, less deserving. I pointed out that in the Sermon on the Mount, Christ was adamant on this point: "For if you love those who love you, what reward have you? Do not even the tax collectors do the same? And if you salute only your brethren, what more are you doing than others? Do not even the Gentiles [heathens] do the same?" No, to be perfected in love, Christ demands we love widely and generously. If Christ is strictly to be believed, then we must extend consideration and care even to future generations and the planet they will inhabit at least in equal proportion to the care we marshal on behalf of our present reality.

Haven't had time to read the Bible? Aren't sure how to balance conservative and liberal thinking? Questioning if you should

LOVE

vote for this or that cause? Ask yourself about the deep character of your proposed choice. Does the side you want to embrace fight for all life? Is it equally concerned with both the born and the unborn, even generations not yet in the womb? Is it available for the deserving and the *undeserving* alike? Is it certain as certain can be yet humble at the same time? In other words, is it perfect love, as defined by Christ in the Sermon on the Mount? That is the central question people must ask if they aim to act wisely despite lacking complete knowledge. And on this, Gregg and I finally agreed.

But even as I was speaking, other questions began to arise because I knew that what I had said was not the whole truth of wise-love. At least, not in a way that was well-defined enough for me to feel comfortable. The Old Testament and its Ten Commandments are great at telling Christians what *not* to do in the name of love. I was left wondering if there was a New Testament equivalent that was equally good at telling Christians what they *should* be doing—a kind of positive version of Christianity to balance the more well-known, thou-shalt-not negative version. Chasing down that and other questions was what lead to the epiphany described in the next chapter.[3]

---

3. This is not to imply that the Old Testament is somehow bad and the New Testament good. It is a matter of approach, like one book rendering portraits of Jesus using pencil versus another book that uses pastels. Both representations portray the same reality, but pencil drawings use shadows (the negative) to reveal the light, whereas pastel drawings focus directly on the light of the world (the positive) and less directly on the shadows—as if to say, focus on the light, and in God's providence the shadows will take care of themselves.

Epiphany and Transformation

IN THE AFTERMATH OF my conversation with Gregg, I wondered if wise-love was just a concept I had made up in the moment to try and express something to a friend or if it had actual, biblical validity beyond the Sermon on the Mount. The epiphany God had foreshadowed in our exchange remained veiled to me until, one day, I realized that the Bible linked wisdom and love in an unmistakably explicit way I had never noticed before. It did so in 1 Corinthians.

Verses from the first two chapters of 1 Corinthians are favorites among many churchgoers—particularly the verses that question, "Where is the wise man? Where is the scribe? Where is the debater of this age? Has not God made foolish the wisdom of the world? For since, in the wisdom of God, the world did not know God through wisdom, it pleased God through the folly of what we preach to save those who believe. For Jews demand signs and Greeks seek [earthly] wisdom, but we preach Christ crucified, a stumbling block to Jews and folly to Gentiles, but to those who are called, both Jews and Greeks, Christ the power of God and the wisdom of God" (1 Cor. 1:20–24).

Yet even as a child, I remember wondering, what was this heavenly wisdom that God was touting? In his holy word, he said things like, "The fear of the Lord is the beginning of wisdom" (Prov. 9:10a). Or, "He who gets wisdom loves himself; he who keeps understanding will prosper" (Prov. 19:8). Or, "Teach us to number our days that we may get a heart of wisdom" (Ps. 90:12). It was clear that God thought wisdom was essential. But over the years, I was left to my own devices regarding what, exactly, the difference was between earthly wisdom and God's wisdom. That is, until a few weeks ago when I realized that the Apostle Paul wrote 1 Corinthians backward.

From the first chapter of Romans, a reader knows that Paul is talking about faith and hope. Sure enough, the book then takes up the theme of faith in Christ and the redemptive hope that comes through our risen Lord. But 1 Corinthians is different. It is almost as if Paul could not wait to get started. In his haste, he uses the first twelve chapters to delve into a variety of topics. Then, in Chapter 13, Paul takes a deep breath, ascertains that he still has not made his point clearly enough, then pens a beautiful description of love. This, Paul explains, has been his point from the start, that the wisdom of God is the wisdom of love.

The problem for me in reading 1 Corinthians 13 has always been that as emotionally poetic as the chapter is, it also seems rather obvious. Who is unaware that love should be patient and kind, not arrogant or rude? We all loosely know what love is, and we all think we are trying to do our reasonable best to live out that love. But if you go back through 1 Corinthians, you will begin to see that keywords in chapter 13, words like *jealousy, arrogant, child,* and *gifts,* work almost like chapter and section headings for everything that comes before and after. In other words, in chapter 13 (traditionally called the *Love Chapter*), Paul is not talking about our generic, everyday, run-of-the-mill understanding of love. He is talking about something precise, something that takes twelve long chapters beforehand and three follow-up chapters to fully describe. The best conception of that idea is wise-love. The holy fusion of these two normally separate visions—the concepts of wisdom and love—infuses the Bible with an enlightened clarity I have seldom experienced since childhood.

Once someone sees this connection, it is hard to unsee that in 1 Corinthians Paul is saying: no matter how wise a person seems by the worldly standards listed in 1 Corinthians 13:1–3, the character of that supposed wisdom will fail the test of time unless it is firmly rooted in the practical, actionable wise-love explicitly defined in the remainder of the Love Chapter.

The Illuminated Bible

The Scriptures use many synonyms for wisdom. The Bible speaks of understanding, knowledge, insight, humility, logos, the spirit, and so on. But in 1 Corinthians, the Apostle Paul clarifies that one universal connection runs like a deep river through the heavenly view of all these words. That universal connection is God's conception of love. What happens if we accept that the Bible is first and foremost about love? What happens if we come to believe that, from beginning to end, the wisdom God is talking about is the wisdom, understanding, and logic of love as explained in the whole of 1 Corinthians and encapsulated in 1 Corinthians 13?

One of the first experiments I did to see if the understanding Paul was preaching in 1 Corinthians made sense was to look at the two versions of the Genesis story, the one in John 1:1–5 and the more well-known version in Genesis 1. Wherever any wisdom-like word appeared, I replaced it with love. What follows is the poetry that resulted from the rewrite of John 1:1–5:

> In the beginning was Love, and Love was with God, and Love was God. From the beginning all things were made through Love, and without the Spirit of Love was not anything made that was made. In this Love was life, and that life was the light of men. That Love still shines in the darkness, and the darkness has not overcome it.

And in Genesis 1:1–2:

> In the beginning God created the heavens and the earth. The earth was without form and void, and darkness was upon the face of the deep; and Love was moving over the face of the waters.

Everywhere I looked, the concept of wise-love deepened the message offered by Scripture from that point onward.

For instance, thinking of Solomon as God's example of the wisest of all kings, I began to wonder why the Bible chose the story of two women arguing over a baby to illustrate his wisdom. There, in a dog-eat-dog world, you had a guy at the apex of greatness—preeminent among military leaders, top-notch in wealth accumulation, the administrative apple of God's eye. Did God choose a story about his strategic brilliance, financial genius, or political acumen as an introductory illustration of his wisdom? No, he told how Solomon suggested chopping a baby in half. This story is not something any earthly king would have picked to highlight. But here—in tones that can suddenly be heard echoing all through Scripture—is why God selected the incident.

When Solomon made his suggestion, one woman said, "Fine, go ahead." The other woman said, "Don't do it. Let the other woman have him. She's the real mother." But Solomon, in his wisdom, realized that the true mother was the one claiming that she was not the mother, and he gave her the child. In other words, the true wisdom of Solomon was that he understood the wisdom of love. He understood that love is not selfish. It "does not insist on its own way," like the woman who did not care which half of the baby she received as long as she received half (1 Cor. 13:5b). He understood that true love "bears all things, believes all things, hopes all things, endures all things" (1 Cor. 13:7). Even to the point of giving up, in the name of love, the child you hold most painfully dear. The story mirrors what Abraham was willing to do to his son in the name of faith and hope and what God was willing to allow for his son because of the world-saving wisdom he vested in love.

This scriptural interpretation reinforces itself when a person notes that Solomon's early wise-loving character was later eclipsed by the unwise love he came to hold for his many wives (over 700, plus 300 concubines). Once he relinquished his fidelity to wise-love, both his fortunes and those of the kingdom of Israel reversed themselves. In 1 Kings 11:30–38, the prophet Ahijah explains to Solomon that because he has forsaken God "and worshiped Ashtoreth the goddess of the Sidonians, Chemosh the god of Moab, and Milcom the god of the Ammonites, and has not walked in my

[God's] ways," God intends to diminish the kingdom of Israel. He means to rip it into eleven tattered pieces and leave the king's son and his descendants with only one small part.

The fullest understanding of large portions of the Bible depends on the insight that God's word is not merely concerned with us having faith and hope. It also wants us to wholeheartedly embrace the added wisdom that comes the moment a person finally realizes that, in the end, it is all about love—love of God and love of others as one's self. If this message is forgotten, then there are places in the Bible where people will not miss merely portions of the Scripture's meaning; they will come away wedded to an understanding that opposes the scriptural intent.

Fail to comprehend that God-defined love and God-defined spiritual wisdom are conceptually the same, and it becomes easy to read and interpret 1 Corinthians 2:15–16 as if it says, "The *man of faith* [it actually says the *spiritual man*] judges all things, but is himself to be judged by no one. 'For who has known the mind of the Lord so as to instruct him?' But *we [who judge ourselves as faithful]* have the mind of Christ."

Based on the certainty many people feel about their faith, they use this verse to claim the right to a religiously supported arrogance. They fail to notice that the next set of verses compares men possessed only of faith to mere "babes in Christ" because their "jealousy and strife" (1 Cor. 3:1, 3) indicates they have failed to display mature, wise-loving spirits (1 Cor. 13:4).

Until a person realizes that the spiritual man and the man on the ground floor of faith are two different beings, it is easy to infer an arrogantly incorrect meaning from this verse. The spiritual man is a wise-loving man, not merely a man of faith. As people begin to near levels of love that bring them closer to being saints than natural men, then and only then should they begin to entertain the notion that this verse applies to them. It is a verse to be aspired to, not to be arrogantly claimed.

All manner of verses throughout the Bible make less sense, make no sense, or tend to give the opposite sense of their actual meaning until we understand the centrality of love and wisdom

LOVE

alloyed. *Yes*, to faith. *Yes*, to hope. But to the greatest of these, to the foundation of Christian thought found in the wisdom of God-ordained love, *Amen!*

Reformation

BACK TO OUR ORIGINAL question: If the Bible, from start to finish, is about wise, peacemaking love, then how did that message get so lost? How did several previous generations of American Christians (and still counting in some places) come to feel that lynching black folks was not just acceptable but ordained by God? The answer hinges on a misunderstanding during the Protestant Reformation.

On the surface, the dispute that initiated the Reformation concerned the selling of indulgences by the Catholic church. By purchasing indulgences (forgiveness for sins), many laypeople came to believe that they could buy their way into heaven with absolute certainty.[1] This misunderstanding was great for church bank accounts. But Martin Luther, the priest who set the Reformation in motion with his ninety-five theses, began to point out that it was not equally great for the spiritual life of Christians. That was the surface question. The deeper and more important question for many Christians was, Could you ever be sure of your ticket to heaven once you could not pay for it?

---

1. English words have a connotation (their intuitive meaning to the average person) and a denotation (their formal dictionary meaning). These two meanings are not always the same. So, too, with Christian theology. What the everyday man on the street believes a biblical passage, practice, or concept means, and what the church intends for it to signify, can be worlds apart. Theologically, the Catholic Church never asserted that indulgences could provide forgiveness apart from a true change of heart. That did not stop many laypeople from interpreting indulgences as carte-blanche forgiveness. Nor did it excuse various priests who failed to vigorously correct this misunderstanding, some even fostering it.

Love

These questions topped the can of worms the thirtieth of Martin Luther's ninety-five theses opened up when it asserted, "Nobody is sure of having repented sincerely enough; much less can he be sure of having received perfect remission of sins."[2] When he wrote Thesis 30, he argued against the belief that by putting a few dollars toward an indulgence, a person could purchase certainty of forgiveness. He was not wrong to argue that point. But once the system of indulgences was overturned, that left a problem.

The difficulty was that indulgences were not necessarily valued for the forgiveness they helped complete as much as for the certainty many people felt they offered. With indulgences gone, where were these believers going to get the assurance they craved? Especially once the church split into Protestant and Catholic factions, both competing for the same souls. If believers could no longer purchase certainty, and the promise of forgiveness offered by the Pope (in his office as the direct spiritual descendant of Peter by apostolic succession) was cut in the schism, how could Protestants be sure they were saved?[3]

Looking to Romans, the theologian John Calvin found the answer that is the basis for certainty in most Protestant churches today: "Therefore, since we are justified by faith, we have peace with God through our Lord Jesus Christ. Through him we have obtained access to this grace in which we stand, and we rejoice in our hope of sharing the glory of God. . . . And hope does not disappoint us, because God's love has been poured into our hearts through the Holy Spirit who has been given to us" (Rom. 5:1–2, 5). Romans 10:10–11, 13 is even more explicit: "For man believes with his heart and so is justified, and he confesses with his lips and so is saved. The Scripture says, 'No one who believes in him will be put

---

2. "95 Theses," para. 30.

3. The desire for certainty in life is not just a modern phenomenon. Consider how quickly the Israelites turned to worshiping the Golden Calf after the uncertainty caused while waiting for Moses to return with the Ten Commandments. Look at the sin committed by King Saul, who just had to know the outcome of a looming battle, to the point that he disregarded God and sought out the medium of Endor so that he could be certain of the future.

to shame.' . . . For, 'everyone who calls upon the name of the Lord will be saved.'"

How strongly is this assurance of certainty felt in many modern Protestant churches? One morning, I decided to test this question by telling my wife a story. I said, "You know how you can get sleepy as can be, and the next thing you know, you're out? When I was younger, I remember falling asleep like that. Occasionally, I would have no idea where I was when I awoke. By the time I recognized my surroundings, I could also see they were dark and deserted. Occasionally, that scared me because I thought, 'Oh, no, the rapture's happened. Everyone is gone, and I've been left behind.'"

Kathleen laughed at my story. Having once been a dyed-in-the-wool Evangelical, she knew exactly what I meant by the rapture. But then I asked her a question: "What's wrong with the story I just told?" She knew immediately and replied, "If you were a real Evangelical, you would be certain that you were saved, so there would have been no way you would wonder about being left behind."

That was precisely the answer I expected because the Good News of the modern gospel has, in many ways, reverted to the same mistake that made the Reformation necessary. Before the Reformation, a *misinterpreted* Catholic Church message could be construed to argue that people could purchase certainty of salvation by paying a few bucks and never considering the actual state of their hearts. In today's post-Reformation world, many Protestant churches purposely or inadvertently assert that people can gain that same certainty by saying a few simple words without daily examining their hearts to see if they truly meant and continue to mean those words. The once-and-done certainty promised by this personal savior/salvation (faith/hope) formulation is now accepted by many people as gospel.

This Good News is not entirely wrong. It is just not entirely right. It overlooks something of both the intent of the original reformers and especially of the Scriptures used to lay the foundation for the Reformation. It is popular these days to say that undeserving people should not receive free government handouts. By the logic of Christians holding this position, such handouts are morally hazardous because, having them in hand, people will then laze their way through life. Yet if that is true, the Good News of free grace offered to all for the price of a few easily uttered words is also morally hazardous.

Worse, whereas society is good at rather cruelly reminding lazy people that they are undeserving moochers, faith-hope Christians are assured by their reading of the Scripture that they are God's specially chosen, the predestined elect (Rom. 8:29–33). Otherwise, they would be unable to utter such words. Nor, according to 1 Corinthians 2:12–16, does anyone get to complain that they are misinterpreting or mishandling the Scriptures because, well, they are spiritual in a way that other people are not.

If this is not a recipe for morally hazardous Christianity, then I do not know what is. It contains the perfect soil and seed for arrogance to grow and converts to feel they can stride about in the world with a sure dominion over whatever ideas and people they wish. That is how many slaveowners managed to square the oppression of their black charges with the God in whom they purported to believe. That is how a lot of people today remain perfectly certain that God loves them the best, even though their hearts are missing any semblance of verifiably expansive love.

Certainty and Control

There is nothing inherently wrong with preferring certainty to uncertainty. Unfortunately, the desire for certainty also tends to link itself to a hunger for control. Difficulties arise the moment people want to be so sure of situational outcomes that they purposely, or inadvertently, wrench control from God and transfer that control to their own hands. Not just control of their own futures, but also undue power over other people's destinies and life outcomes. This desire for control happens frequently enough that it is fair to wonder if many people gravitate toward their preferred religious narratives less because of the certainty it gives them about heaven to come and more because of the control it allows them to justify and exert over others on earth.

In a meritocratic society, the faith-hope gospel lends itself perfectly to pointing fingers at the *wrong* type of people. Good outcomes are equated with good people and bad outcomes with bad people. The biblical admonition to hate what is wrong becomes a recipe for hating people themselves as society passes judgment on those they perceive as less faithful, less righteous, less deserving. Why should adherents to such a gospel reach out to help the poor, the addicted, the imprisoned, the outcasts, the rejects? Why do anything at all if it is unnecessary for faith and hope to be accompanied by a gracious, redeeming love that seeks to look past the judgmental conviction of law?

But the true gospel, even as presented in the last third of Romans, is not the Good News of faith and hope alone. It is the even better news of faith, hope, and love. Believing only in the faith-hope version of the gospel is like being someone who hears Christ knock, knock, knocking at their front door. But when that person finally answers the call, opens the door, and steps through into hope . . . she stops. There she sits on the front porch, never realizing the real reason for Christ's knocking was the hope that she would go into the world with him on a journey of love.

The situation is like a slightly different version of that old joke where a person finds himself at the pearly gates asking why God overlooked trying to save him when his home was flooding. But in the new faith-hope-love version, God replies, "I did try and save you! Three times! I sent my son with a jet ski, a boat, and a helicopter to ask if you wanted to go with me to help others. But every time you said, 'No, I'm going to wait for the ride that goes directly to dry land.'"

The faith-hope gospel can make us fit for the lowest reaches of heaven. But there is something about God's love that, as we use it to help others, also helps us. It brings a little bit of heaven to earth even before we arrive. And when we do get there, it makes us among the kingdom's greats.[4]

4. In Matthew 18, the disciples pose the question to Jesus, "Who is the

LOVE

The Necessity of the Faith, Hope, Love Narrative

If a pastor were to ask the average parishioner the topic of last week's sermon or, God forbid, the message a month ago, most people would be unable to recall it. That is not necessarily bad because people tend to look to events, stories, and sermons to confirm their narratives. As long as the sermon fits neatly into the narrative, the narrative will be strengthened, but the story will often be forgotten, one more drop in a worldview bucket that is already full to overflowing.

The problem with the faith-hope narrative is that most people already think they are reasonably loving. Even most slaveowners believed that. But the central Christian question has never been about whether Christians should love in the name of Christ. It has always been about what, exactly, God means by love and what we should do with that love once embraced. Christians need to know precisely what they are aiming at if they are to direct their lives toward that target. Every mission-oriented book in existence preaches that the more clearly we define our goals, the more likely we are to reach them.

The faith-hope-love narrative, especially the love portion of that narrative, needs to be at the vanguard of a new reformation of the church and our individual lives. Any narrative that fails to focus specifically on the meaning and use of God's love leaves that question open to be answered however a person wants.[5] Often that

---

greatest in the kingdom of heaven?" Jesus explains that "whoever humbles himself like this child, he is the greatest in the kingdom of heaven. Whoever receives one such child in my name receives me." In light of this parable, it is interesting to note how some people like to think of themselves as *the grown-ups in the room* and how those same people often have a habit of dehumanizing others by referring to them as *boy* (toward black men) or *babe* (for someone a guy might wish to bed) or *the little woman* (in reference to the wife at home with the kids). As Wordsworth said, every child comes from heaven, "trailing clouds of glory." That child resides in each of us, glory included, if we are humble enough to admit it. As we do unto that child and other children, so we do also unto Christ. So, too, do we ascend or descend on the hierarchy of heaven's scale of greatness.

5. This same argument is presented by Calvin in the Institutes of the

love gets turned around into a love of self, community, tribe, or nation—never going beyond the front porch. Worse still, when challenged by a pastor or fellow Christian on a point of love, the faith-hope narrative equips them with the ready reply, "Hey, I'm already saved. I'm filled with the spirit, too. What I'm doing and thinking must be right. So quit judging me."

Reminding people of the complete faith-hope-love narrative and the Bible's original intent does not automatically mean a sudden focus on understanding the particulars of how Christians can treat immigrants better, how we can be more respectful of black lives, or how we can be more sensitive to women's issues or minority concerns. As a math teacher, if every time I gave my students a slightly different math problem I then found myself having to explain the particulars of that new problem, I would eventually realize that the difficulty is not in the particular. It is not that my students do not know how to do this or that problem; it is that they do not know how to do math.

Same, too, in Christianity. If people have learned what Christ means by love, then the specific applications of the more universal principle should need little explanation after a while. When time and again the church finds itself having to preach to specifics, that points to the more general problem that the centrality of love in the faith-hope-love trinity has been lost. It is not that people do not want to be better at math or to be more loving. It is more often true that they do not know what they are aiming at or how to get there.

In a purposeful echo of the wording in Luther's theses, 96) We, the people, need to be taught again what wise-love is. 97) We need to understand that faith and hope are not the end of a journey. They are the beginning. 98) We need to remember that the Good News does not stop at the front porch but is about opening the door of faith and hope so we can journey into the heart of God's love for others. 99) We need to view love in a way that is so well-defined that its tenets and the types of actions those tenets

---

Christian Religion, chapter 6, but with regard to God rather than God-ordained love.

LOVE

invite us into are every bit as familiar as the Lord's Prayer or the Nicaean creed. 100) We need to realize that faith and hope will get a person into heaven but only onto the ground floor, only into steerage class, only in the children's section. If we would be greatest in the kingdom of heaven, then 101) we need to seek a soul full of grace, a heart filled with the goodness of God's wise-love—doing on earth as our faith tells us we can one day hope to do in heaven.[6]

First Corinthians is the perfect book to frame the Bible and to center the Christian walk in such love. But before we dive into that portion of Paul's writings, it is helpful to ask one more question: Why is the character of Romans so different from that of 1 Corinthians when it comes to talking about the details of Christian love?

---

6. "Drum Major Instinct," para. 2.

Rome Versus Corinth
A New Foundation

ROMANS IS INDEED DIFFERENT in character from 1 Corinthians, but why? The answer is partially due to the difference in Paul's relationship with each church before he began writing his letters. But the more significant reason for the difference is how each church's historical and cultural circumstances shaped the concerns they were asking Paul to address.

Regarding personal influences, Paul's relationship to the church in Rome was less intimate than his relationship with the church in Corinth. Historians are unsure who founded the Roman church. It was vibrant, large, and strategically important to the spread of the faith.[1] But it was not Paul's flesh and blood, so to speak.

By contrast, Paul helped found the church in Corinth and was instrumental in its growth over the years. When he wrote his letter to the Romans, most historians believe he wrote it from Corinth. Paul cared about the Roman church. But he did so in the abstract, like a person might care about a sponsored child he has never shared a meal with or even met. By comparison, Paul loved the church in Corinth. He loved it with an intimacy born from years of close, personal involvement in the life of that community.

One cannot help but wonder if these two realities tilted his letter to the Romans slightly toward the intellectual, theological

---

1. O'Neal, "Earliest Days," paras. 8, 21.

side of the house while lending his first letter to the Corinthians a more emotionally intimate feel. The degree to which this supposition is true is hard to say. But many theologians have noticed the difference in tone between the two books and conjecture this might be the case.

Far less of a conjecture are the verifiable events that shaped the church in Rome while leaving Corinth relatively untouched. These varied histories profoundly influenced the problems with which each church needed help. When Protestant and Catholic churches chose the book of Romans over 1 Corinthians as their theological underpinning, the Christian world inherited a theology substantially more prepared to deal with problems like those that plagued the Romans and less prepared to handle the types of issues with which the Corinthians grappled.

Rome and the Accidental Gospel of the Western World

Although referred to as the Church in Rome, that *church* was actually a collection of smaller house churches. Culturally, these small churches had a distinctly Jewish feel to them because, at least initially, their congregations were primarily Jews. That changed when Claudius, the fourth emperor of Rome, banished Jews from the city for five years, from 49 AD until he died in 54 AD.[2]

When Nero ascended the throne after the death of Claudius, he allowed his predecessor's edict to lapse. Upon the Jewish Christians' return to Rome, they found that the Gentiles had necessarily assumed control of church affairs. The situation they found reminds me of what it was like for many families when I was in the Navy. Guys would head off on nine-month or year-long cruises. While they were gone, their wives were left entirely in charge of family affairs. When the husbands finally returned, there was often a remarkable amount of friction. The guys immediately wanted their houses to run the way they had just before their departure,

---

2. Berding, "Something about Romans," para. 1.

not the way their wives were running them after a multitude of practical considerations and changes their husbands had not been a part of negotiating.

The same thing happened in Rome. Perspectives and ways of doing that were precious to the Jews and integral to an understanding of the theological underpinnings of Christianity weakened in the intervening years. Gentile practices and perspectives, though not necessarily erasing in full that of their Jewish counterparts, evolved without having to grapple with how to integrate them fully. When Paul finally wrote his letter to the Romans, this was the situation he was addressing: balancing a Jewish understanding of the foundational law and prophets with a Gentile tradition that was more familiar with and understanding of the concepts of grace and faith.[3] Like the Navy husband with his wife, they had to re-establish the hows and whys of day-to-day belief, ritual, and community.

In this vein, Romans is a beautiful piece of explanatory writing. Divided roughly into thirds, the first two-thirds of the book deals with faith and hope, while the last third finishes up by concentrating on love. But there is a considerable problem with Romans as read in the West: For many readers, the first two-thirds of Romans provides the theological basis for being saved and getting into heaven. It explains that there is no longer a need to sacrifice unblemished lambs for our sins because Christ is the Lamb of God offered for all of us. Now we can have a direct, personal relationship with Christ as our high priest with no need of any other intercessor. All we have to do is accept Christ as our personal Lord and Savior, and by faith, we will be saved.

From there, I would challenge many Christians to tell me what comes next without peeking. A few of the most oft-repeated verses? Something those chapters definitively ask us not to do? An accounting of why we owe no man or woman anything but *this*? Which people are and are not supposed to be society's rightful judges?

---

3. Berding, "Something about Romans," para. 6.

Forget this last one-third of Romans, and what do you have left? You get the perfect theology for the West—the accidental gospel of Christian individualism. It comes with one personalized relationship to the Lord and Savior, one individually guaranteed invite into heaven, and no need to read or think much beyond those points. Was that Paul's intent in writing the book? Absolutely not. However, drop Romans into a populace that prizes individual or tribal concerns more than interpersonal or united concerns, and should anyone be surprised that is the takeaway?

We get a theology, but not a Christology. We get an intellectual idea of what to believe so that it counts as a checkmark of faith. But how to take that faith and grow it to maturity? How to take that interior faith—that head-faith or professed faith—and incarnate it so that it lives and breathes and walks around in the exterior world doing widely recognizable good beyond our communities? Less so. How to talk about people we have hardly met besides seeing them on TV or in the newspaper? Sure. How to love them in the up-close, daily, communally personal way spoken of in 1 Corinthians? Not so much.

It is impossible to effectively contrast the difference between the headspace of a theology and the hands, feet, and heart space of a Christology without adding a description of life in Corinth to the mix. So it is time for a brief look at Corinth.

Corinth and the Purposeful Gospel of Community

There is no understanding Paul's first letter to the Corinthians without correctly understanding Corinth. Corinth never experienced an edict that expelled its Jews. It was originally a Greek city and remained a cosmopolitan society that accepted virtually all comers. Whereas Rome was the Roman Empire's political capital and was more like Washington D.C, Corinth (a port city) was a Greek center of commerce most reminiscent of modern-day New York City. It was avowedly dedicated to the financial bottom line and to a level of sexual promiscuity that would make New Yorkers either blush or turn green with envy. German theologian Ernst von Dobschütz is quoted as describing the place like this:

> The ideal of the Corinthian was the reckless development of the individual. The merchant who made his gain by all and every means, the man of pleasure surrendering himself to every lust, the athlete steeled to every bodily exercise and proud in his physical strength, are the true Corinthian types: in a word the man who recognised [sic] no superior and no law but his own desires.[4]

It is easy to pigeonhole ancient Corinth as a center of depraved, secular excesses that were every bit the equal of the way many Christians characterize modern-day New York. But that would miss the point because Corinth's most important commodity was not excess. It was excellence. If you were an athlete, you wanted to win the Isthmian Games, which took place in Corinth every two years, both the year before and after Rome's Olympics. If you were a financier, you had better be prepared to work like a fiend raking in embarrassing amounts of drachma during the day, then able to party all night with the best of them, then ready to rinse and repeat, again and again, often with little to no sleep.

When I think of Corinth, I think of one evening I spent with my friend Jim Carpenter while we both trained for the Olympics. In many German training centers, carbo-loading means drinking beer after an intense session of exercise and competition. That is how we found ourselves underground one night in the training center's self-serve bar—beers in hand but without a bottle opener. The lack of an opener was no deterrent to Jim. Within seconds, he had his bottle open with a trick I had never seen before. Then mine, too.

When I asked him how he had come by his technique, he explained that he had once intended to be a priest. Eventually, he changed his mind. But, as he related matters, his change of mind did not produce a change in ethic. He figured that if he was no longer going to be the most excellent priest possible, he was at least

---

4 Parry, *First Epistle of Paul*, IX.

going to be the most exceptional guy possible. By his way of thinking, step one on that list meant never, ever being in a situation where you could not handily open an ice-cold beer and partake of its virtues. That was the ethic of Jim Carpenter and Corinth: excellence in all things, though not always the things to which Christian souls might be presumed to aspire.

In terms of external concerns, this made Corinth an interesting place to build a church. In Corinth, people who talked the talk but failed to walk the walk did not last long. Inhabitants had little patience for blowhards, religious or otherwise. In Corinth, paying lip service to Christian love was not good enough. You actually (note the similarity between the words *actually* and *actions*) had to be loving, in the most consistently excellent sense of the word. This proximity to a culture of daily excellence meant the church problems in Corinth were less theological and more about how to be in such a world "without being of the world."

Given that the Corinthian church included Latins, Greeks, Asians, and Jews, as well as Egyptians and Syrians,[5][6] questions about giving fair voice to all adherents of the faith abounded. The challenge was how to give due respect to and address the needs of varying cultural heritages, philosophical outlooks, prior religious traditions, and spiritual maturity levels without sacrificing the heart of the Christian faith.

There was also the problem of dissuading people from forming cults of personality around influencers and, instead, asking them to let the spirit of Christian love be the dominant influence. How should people carry themselves externally as part of the culture? How should they behave internally as a part of the church body? These were the questions Paul was dealing with in Corinth. He was concerned not just with racking up professions of faith but with fostering a community whose wise-loving actions truly spoke louder than words—deafeningly, excellently so.

---

5. "Corinth," para. 2.
6. Parry, *First Epistle of Paul*, pg. VIII.

But What About the Pilgrims?

Americans like to think of themselves, too, as exceptional. That continued belief is fertilized by the nation's favorite narratives, including tales of the Pilgrims. But did you know that persecution was not the main reason the Pilgrims ended up in the United States? They were indeed persecuted. But before coming to America, many of them first settled in the Netherlands. There they were completely free from English persecution. So why risk life and limb to sail thousands of miles to America when the Dutch already welcomed them with open arms?

It turns out that the Dutch did not just welcome them; they also welcomed everyone else and the ideas that came with them. Similar to New York and Corinth, Amsterdam was also a cosmopolitan port city. Unfortunately, the original Pilgrims did not just want freedom from persecution or even freedom in general. What they wanted most was isolation from the rich wealth of cultural temptations they felt would be a poor influence on their adherents. They had absolutely no interest in being "in the world"; they preferred segregation from the world. That is why they finally came to America. They wanted to remain pure and apart from what they considered polluting influences.[7]

After finally reading a complete account of their journey, I began to wonder, What good is a religion that lacks faith in its ability to compete in the broader culture fairly? What good is faith if it is comfortable only in gated communities and isolated spaces, or a religion that is great at negative words for everyone else but short on recognizably excellent, positive examples of themselves loving and being in the larger world?

Just because this or that person's version of excellence fails to accord with our own does not make them any less excellent. On the contrary, it testifies to their integrity. Excellence in their chosen endeavors gives them reasonable cause to ask if they can see matching excellence in the finger-pointers or attractive integrity in anyone wishing to proselytize them. Otherwise, they are left

7. Woodard, *American Nations*, 68

looking at us like the person who failed to make an Olympic team but who, nonetheless, feels comfortable criticizing someone else for winning a gold medal in a sport the critic despises.

What, Then, Is a Christian to Do?

From the time of the Pilgrims onward, Americans were always able to move someplace new. They could pick places where competition to their ideas and preferred way of life was minimal. Whether people were heeding the call to head westward, migrate to the suburbs, or remain in small towns, America has always had its getaways and *keep-aways*. But as Reinhold Niebuhr observed in *The Irony of American History*, the curse of so much space was that American Christendom would never know its true character until there was no place left to which to escape.

Writing just after the time of Hitler, Niebuhr understood that Germany's call for more room to live, more *lebensraum*, was a call in precisely the opposite direction of the one for which Paul called. Both Niebuhr and Paul believed that the better idea, the Christian ideal, was to make more room in our hearts for others instead of less room for them in *our* spaces. Until the same *lebensraum* choice unavoidably confronted Americans themselves, Niebuhr felt there was no predicting what the character of American Christianity would reveal itself to be.

Listening to recent burgeoning calls to colonize the moon or Mars, the thoughtful Christian has to wonder if the history that led the Puritans west is repeating itself. Whether subconsciously or consciously, it is as if many of us would prefer outer space over having the *wrong* kind of people in our personal spaces. Our sudden wish to settle these long-dead spheres seems almost Freudian. It is as if we are acknowledging in advance that we are killing our world because too many of us have to have our own individual ways. Whether person to person (narcissism), state to state (confederalism), tribe to tribe (tribalism), religion to religion (fascism), or nation to nation (nationalism), too much of today's American Christianity displays a character that seems desperate to avoid sacrificing to Christ to make room in its heart for people it does not want there.

Romans was and should be the theological center of the Christian faith. It points Christians squarely in the direction of faith and hope. It beautifully explains what we should think about our religion and what we should say to explain it to non-Christians. But suppose people desire a faith that moves beyond the intellectual, beyond the emotionally distant, into the actionable heart of Christian community and embodied love. In that case, they should look to 1 Corinthians as the Christological center of the Bible. Romans is great for coming to a personal, individualized relationship with the God of faith and hope. But for those seeking maturity in the practical, everyday demands of Christian love and nurturing community, 1 Corinthians is a must.

Faith, Hope, but Especially Love
A New Religious Narrative

RATHER THAN APPEARING TO impose my own interpretation on the whole of 1 Corinthians as it relates to the thirteenth chapter, I would first like to let God's Word speak for itself. To that end, I divided chapter thirteen into its ten principal themes. Each theme becomes a major topic heading in my outline. Under each heading, verses are included from the full text of 1 Corinthians that speak directly to that topic. This progression ensures that each topic phrase is tightly defined in the way Paul meant it to be understood instead of how we might intuitively believe he meant it. This structure helps replace personal, gut-level feelings about love with a biblically defined love.

Only two points need mentioning before letting the Scriptures speak for themselves. First, when looking for example verses on wisdom, I did a computer search and noticed there were, in fact, two verses that capture the entire spirit of 1 Corinthians. One was James 3:17 (NIV): "But the wisdom that comes from heaven is first of all pure; then peace-loving, considerate, submissive, full of mercy and good fruit, impartial and sincere." This list strongly echoes the Sermon on the Mount, where Christ says blessed are the pure in heart, the peacemakers, the meek, the merciful. It also parallels the spirit in which Paul wrote 1 Corinthians. Thus, the tenets of wise-love found in 1 Corinthians can also be thought of as peacemaking love.

The other striking observation I made while searching through verses on wisdom was the prevalence of calls for humility, including the need for humility in its less recognizable form, fear. This emphasis is echoed in 1 Corinthians, where I came away with the distinct impression that true love, wise-love, the peacemaking love that God desires us to exhibit, is not possible without humility.

The Ten Defining Themes of Christian Love

- **THEME 1**: *No matter what else people have to their credit, if they have not love, then they have nothing.*
    a. Principle: The only measure of merit God will accept is a merit based on how loving people are toward God, as evidenced by their love for others and themselves.
    b. 1 Cor. 13:1–3. If I speak in the tongues of men and of angels, but have not love, I am a noisy gong or a clanging cymbal. And if I have prophetic powers, and understand all mysteries and all knowledge, and if I have all faith so as to remove mountains, but have not love, I am nothing. If I give away all I have, and if I deliver my body to be burned, but have not love, I gain nothing.
        i. This verse captures the soul of the matter. When Paul talks about earthly wisdom, he is talking about loveless wisdom. True wisdom is found in understanding the ins and outs of being a loving person and then actually following through by spreading God's love as we act as his hands, heart, and feet in the world.
- **THEME 2**: *Love is patient and kind.*
    a. Principle: As ambassadors of God, we must always keep the needs of others in mind—their need for care, encouragement, and grace—so that they experience God's love through us.

LOVE

B. 1 Cor. 10:23–27, 31–33. "All things are lawful," but not all things are helpful. "All things are lawful," but not all things build up. Let no one seek his own good, but the good of his neighbor. Eat whatever is sold in the meat market without raising any questions on the ground of conscience. For "the earth is the Lord's and everything in it." If one of the unbelievers invites you to dinner and you are disposed to go, eat whatever is set before you without raising any questions on the ground of conscience. . . . So, whether you eat or drink, or whatever you do, do all to the glory of God. Give no offense to Jews or to Greeks or to the church of God, just as I try to please all men in everything I do, not seeking my own advantage, but that of many, that they may be saved. Be imitators of me, as I am of Christ.

   i. There is no better description of *divine kindness* and the reasons we should be motivated to show it.

- **THEME 3**: *Love is not jealous or boastful.*

   a. Principle: We should not be religiously tribal or socially tribal because we feel one tribe or person is better or more exceptional than another in God's eyes. It may seem so in our eyes, but we are all beggars at the door of grace in God's eyes.

   b. 1 Cor. 3:1–4. But I, brethren, could not address you as spiritual men, but as men of the flesh, as babes in Christ. I fed you with milk, not solid food; for you were not ready for it; and even yet you are not ready, for you are still of the flesh. For while there is jealousy and strife among you, are you not of the flesh, and behaving like ordinary men? For when one says, "I belong to Paul," and another, "I belong to Apollos," are you not merely men?

   c. 1 Cor. 4:6–7. I have applied all this to myself and Apollos for your benefit, brethren, that you may learn by us not to go beyond what is written, that none of you may be puffed up in favor of one against another. For who sees anything different in you? What have you that you did not receive? If then you received it, why do you boast as if it were not a gift?

    d. 1 Cor. 12:12–15. For just as the body is one and has many members, and all the members of the body, though many are one body, so it is with Christ. For by one Spirit we were all baptized into one body—Jews or Greeks, slaves or free—and all were made to drink of one Spirit. For the body does not consist of one member but of many. If the foot should say, "Because I am not a hand, I do not belong to the body," that would not make it any less a part of the body.

- **THEME 4**: *Love is not arrogant or rude.*

  a. Principle: Arrogance goes hand in hand with judgment. They are two sides of the same coin. Insofar as possible, let God be the judge of peoples' actions. But if we must judge, then we should choose to judge ourselves and love outsiders.

  b. 1 Cor. 5:9–12. I wrote to you in my letter not to associate with immoral men; not at all meaning the immoral of this world, or the greedy and robbers, or idolaters, since then you would need to go out of the world. But rather I wrote to you not to associate with anyone who bears the name of brother if he is guilty of immorality or greed, or is an idolater, reviler, drunkard, or robber—not even to eat with such a one. For what have I to do with judging outsiders? Is it not those inside the church whom you are to judge? God judges those outside. "Drive out the wicked person from among you."

      i. If you are pointing out a speck in someone else's eye, there is probably a log in your own (Matt. 7:3).

      ii. An extended version of the same discussion takes place in Romans 1–2.

a. 1 Cor. 4:18. Some are arrogant, as though I were not coming to you. But, I will come to you soon, if the Lord wills, and I will find out not the talk of these arrogant people but their power. For the kingdom of God does not consist in talk but in power [the power of God's love lived out].

- **THEME 5**: *Love does not insist on its own way.*
    a. Principle: Wise-love acts as an ambassador, a peacemaker.
    b. 1 Cor. 6:12. "All things are lawful for me," but not all things are helpful.
        i. Chapter 6 is about who will cede to avoid disputes and keep the peace. True Christians are peacemakers who, in the name of God's love, are gracious enough to forego insisting on their own way as they search for compromise and the common good.
    c. 1 Cor. 9:19–22: For though I am free from all men, I have made myself a slave to all, that I might win the more. To the Jews I became as a Jew, in order to win Jews; to those under the law I became as one under the law—though not being myself under the law—that I might win those under the law. To those outside the law I became as one outside the law—not being without law toward God but under the law of Christ—that I might win those outside the law. To the weak I became weak, that I might win the weak. I have become all things to all men, that I might by all means save some. I do it for the sake of the gospel, that I may share in its blessings.
        i. In a country with a long legacy of slavery, many people want nothing to do with the notion of becoming slaves to all, of subverting their freedom for the good of someone else or the broader society.

- **THEME 6**: *Love is not irritable or resentful.*
    a. Principle: Wise-love does not expect a return on investment beyond furthering the kingdom of God, nor does it get irritable or resentful when a personal return is not forthcoming.
    b. 1 Cor. 9:1–18, but quoting only verse 18. *What then is my reward? Just this: that in my preaching I may make the gospel free of charge, not making full use of my right in the gospel.*
        i. In this single verse, Paul talks about the right to be compensated for the job he is doing. But in the tone of the entire section surrounding this verse, I am reminded of how a person sometimes gives a smile, opens a door, or does the right thing, but then feels irritable or resentful if the smile is not returned, if a thank you is not said for the opened door, if other people profit from wrongdoing even while we suffer for doing right. "Do not be irritable or resentful when earthly returns are not full-coming," Paul seems to be saying. "We are building up our treasures in heaven, and we will find our reward there."

- **THEME 7**: *Love does not rejoice in the wrong.*
    a. Principle: Do not rejoice while filled with lies and hypocrisy; rather, rejoice when filled with sincerity and truth. In this phrase, Paul ties arrogance to overlooking the truth of who we really are—unavoidably fallen creatures at every turn. That oversight allows us to find a joyful self-satisfaction in the illusion of our goodness, especially when compared to what we perceive as the shortcomings of others.
    b. 1 Cor. 5:1–2, 6–8. *It is actually reported that there is immorality among you, and of a kind that is not found even among pagans; for a man is living with his father's wife. And you are arrogant! Ought you not rather to mourn?*

LOVE

. . . Cleanse out the old leaven that you may be a new lump, as you really are unleavened. For Christ, our paschal lamb, has been sacrificed. Let us, therefore, celebrate the festival, not with the old leaven, the leaven of malice and evil, but with the unleavened bread of sincerity and truth.

- **THEME 8**: *Love bears all things, believes all things, hopes all things, endures all things.*
    - a. Principle: Love is externally meek but internally indomitable for the sake of Christ.
    - b. 1 Cor. 4:9, 11–13. For I think that God has exhibited us apostles as last of all, like men sentenced to death. . . . To the present hour we hunger and thirst, we are ill-clad and buffeted and homeless, and we labor, working with our own hands. When reviled, we bless; when persecuted, we endure; when slandered, we try to conciliate; we have become, and are now, as the refuse of the world, the offscouring of all things.
        - i. Reading this verse makes me think of the Negro spirituals that came from slaves in the deep South. Those spirituals capture the attitude necessary for survival amid service. They echo the philosophy we are supposed to embrace as servants in Christ and spreaders of peace and love.
    - c. 1 Cor. 9:23–27. I do it all for the sake of the gospel, that I may share in its blessings. Do you not know that in a race all the runners compete, but only one receives the prize? So run that you may obtain it. Every athlete exercises self-control in all things. They do it to receive a perishable wreath, but we an imperishable. Well, I do not run aimlessly, I do not box as one beating the air; but I pommel my body and subdue it, lest after preaching to others I myself should be disqualified.

i. This verse makes all the more sense when we remember that Corinth was home to the renowned Isthmian Games. Taking place every two years, the competition attracted the best athletes in the ancient world. They would undoubtedly have been part of the crowd when Paul spoke. People in the city would also have been familiar with the grueling training they endured to be among the best athletes. They provided the perfect metaphor for what it takes to pursue excellence in Christian love.

- **THEME 9**: *Love is not childish or immature.*

  a. Principle: The mature Christian has cultivated a capacity for love. The childlike Christian is closer to the natural man. Such a person remains in the nursery, on the ground floor, in the steerage class of faith and self-centered hope, as opposed to having embraced an expansive, compassionate, world-changing love.

  b. 1 Cor. 2:15–3:4. The spiritual man judges all things, but is himself to be judged by no one. 'For who has known the mind of the Lord so as to instruct him?' But we have the mind of Christ. But I, brethren, could not address you as spiritual men, but as men of the flesh, as babes in Christ. I fed you with milk, not solid food; for you were not ready for it; and even yet you are not ready, for you are still of the flesh. For while there is jealousy and strife among you, are you not of the flesh, and behaving like ordinary men? For when one says, "I belong to Paul," and another, "I belong to Apollos," are you not merely men?

     i. We are asked not to act tribally or in a cliquish manner.

  c. 1 Cor. 12:7. To each is given the manifestation of the Spirit for the common good.

> i. It is childishly selfish to use Christ's love *only* for one's personal comfort and benefit. It is meant for the common good as well.

- **THEME 10**: *Wise-love acknowledges that now we see in a mirror dimly and only in part.*
  - a. Principle: Absolute, black-and-white, unyielding certainty that fails to give even a modicum of credence to outsiders' perspectives is a sign of people who are lacking in Christian wisdom, grace, and love.
  - b. 1 Cor. 4:1. This is how one should regard us, as servants of Christ and stewards of the mysteries of God.
  - c. 1 Cor. 8:1–2. Now concerning food offered to idols; we know that "all of us possess knowledge." "Knowledge" puffs up, but love builds up. If anyone imagines that he knows something, he does not know as he ought to know. But if one loves God [and so others], one is known by him.

- **THEME 1, REPRISED**: *Faith, hope, and love abide, these three, but the greatest of these is love.*
  - a. Principle: The highest wisdom of God is the wisdom of love in all things.
  - b. 1 Cor. 1:19. For it is written, "I will destroy the wisdom of the wise, and the cleverness of the clever I will thwart."
    - i. "The wisdom of the wise, and the cleverness of the clever" alludes to rational, utilitarian, bottom-line knowledge, understanding, and wisdom that discounts the central importance of peacemaking love as a dependable guiding principle.
  - c. 1 Cor. 1:22–25. For Jews demand signs and Greeks seek wisdom, but we preach Christ crucified, a stumbling block to Jews and folly to Gentiles, but to those who are called, both Jews and Greeks, Christ the power of God and the wisdom of God. For the foolishness of God is

wiser than men, and the weakness of God is stronger than men.

- i. To many onlookers, the death of Christ was a sure sign of the stupidity of love in a world where power, the bottom-line, and tribal self-interest seemed, yet again, to have won out.
- ii. The resurrection of Christ is God's counterargument to this perspective. It proves that the love of God is wiser than men, and the power of God—even when muted as he loves the world through us—is stronger than men and even death.

d. 1 Cor. 16:13. Be watchful, stand firm in your faith, be courteous, be strong. Let all that you do be done in love.

- i. Paul concludes 1 Corinthians with an emphasis on love. This close is a mini-version of 1 Corinthians 13 and a summary of the intent behind the whole chapter.

It is also a fitting rule by which to take the measure of our personal walks with Christ: Would outsiders judge us as always courteous and kind? If they had to guess, would they think we do everything in the name of love? Forgetting every other measure by which we might assign merit to ourselves, would onlookers know we are Christians by the quality and character of our love as described in 1 Corinthians and throughout the Bible?

Faith, Hope, but Especially Love, Paraphrased

THE BIBLE IS NOT a dead book. The breath of God is alive and well within it. That indwelling—the Spirit of love—converses with the voice of every age. Of the Christian, it asks, Are you what a humble, merciful person looks like in such a time and place? Of the nation, Is this how a patient, generous, redemptive police force, school system, or society manifests itself? In each era, the dialogue and the answers it yields are different and the same, all at once.

What might that conversation sound like if Paul could pen 1 Corinthians 13 for this American moment? To my mind, it would sound something like this: You have heard it said that if I speak in the tongues of men—whether speaking Spanish, English, or some other language—or even if I speak as the angels, if I have not love, I am a noisy gong or a clanging cymbal. You have heard that if I have prophetic powers and understand all mysteries and all knowledge, and if I have all faith so as to remove mountains, if I have not love, I am nothing.

It is true. It makes no difference how smart I am, how big my house is, what job title I have, or how much I earn; if I have not love, I deserve nothing. I could be tops on whatever meritocratic scale society sets up to judge winners and losers, but without love, all my supposed merit is worthless.

Love is patient and kind. It does not go around bragging that it is real and others are not real. It does not assume it is exceptional and others are less so because that would be arrogant and rude.

Love is not jealous. It does not boast that this cafe counter, this bus seat, this space, land, or nation belongs to it and it alone. Nor is love irritable or resentful, believing it is losing something whenever someone else gains a seat at the counter, on the bus, or at table. For this land is not ours but God's. Not even our bodies are our own. They were bought with a price, and if we are Christians, they are the Holy Spirit's personal property and meant to be temples of love (1 Cor. 6:19).

Such love does not insist on its own way because wise-love is meant to meet others where they are, not where the presumption that often masquerades as love thinks they should be. In trying to meet others where they are, wise-love is a dreamer. It does not say, "Forget the attempt because heaven on earth is impossible." It is willing to bear, believe, hope, and endure all things, even if the end of that effort means only one more small step toward God's will being done on earth as it is in heaven.

Any honest attempt at such love knows how far short of fullness it is falling. It understands that even now, even having passed through the door of faith, we see through a mirror dimly. It realizes that in every moment we are at risk of acting more like the fractious child described in 1 Corinthians 3 and less like the wise-loving adult at the end of 1 Corinthians 2. For our knowledge of what it means to love in this way and our prophecy in the name of such love are imperfect. But when the perfect comes, the imperfect will pass away. Now we know in part, then we will understand in full, even as we have been fully understood.

So, faith, hope, and love abide. The faith of Abraham, the hope of Christ, and the love of the Spirit, these three abide. But the greatest of these—the beginning, middle, and end of the journey—resides in love.

The Tenets of Wise-Love

1. Wise-love judges and acts in the name of mercy and grace rather than on behalf of earthly measures of worth or deservedness.

2. Wise-love is patient and kind. As if a peacemaker or peacekeeper on loan from God, it attempts to meet people where they are.

3. Wise-love is not jealous or boastful. It has enough understanding to neither believe in nor boast about being more exceptional, more excellent, more real, or more deserving than other people in the eyes of God. It is never jealous, as if it has something to lose due to ownership, for it is ever conscious that all it has in this world is a gift from God.

4. Wise-love is not arrogant or rude. In humility, if it must judge, then it judges itself before others. And when doing so, it judges only those in its own religious tribe and never those of another persuasion. With the attitude of an emissary, it understands that the temptation to judge should signal the need to begin questioning, listening, and serving, not demeaning.

5. Wise-love does not insist on its own way. Not on its own religious rituals, social traditions, preferred pew, or methods of approach. For the sake of spreading God's wise-love, it is flexible in all things nonessential to living as a loving person.

The Tenets of Wise-Love

6. Wise-love is not irritable or resentful. It does not grow tired of doing the right thing just because others are not doing it. It is not dissuaded from service because it is hard or because no one but God is saying thank you. Wise-love may get angry, but it does not sin. It looks for healthy ways to keep a graceful soul untinged by bitterness.

7. Wise-love does not rejoice in the wrong but rejoices in the right. It is not hypocritical. It does not cast the first or even second stone because it understands how people and tribes tend to discount the significance of their own sins while magnifying the sins of others.

8. Wise-love bears all things, believes all things, hopes all things, and endures all things. It has the mature, persistent spirituality of an adult who knows that victory seldom comes without faith-testing defeats. It is childlike but not childish in still believing God's love always prevails, even over death.

9. Nor does wise-love reason in childish ways. It does not believe it knows everything and can judge everyone while still on this side of heaven. For those who are wisest in love, like those greatest in understanding, are ever more humbled by the realization that the better they get at loving and understanding others, the further they have to go.

10. So, faith, hope, and love abide, these three. But the greatest of these is love—the love of God that is the foundation of faith and hope, plus the love of neighbor as if one's self. This is the sum and greatness of all God's wisdom.

Love and the Ten Commandments

ANY DISCUSSION OF WISE-LOVE remains incomplete without talking about the Ten Commandments. In Mark 12, when Christ is asked to name the greatest commandment, he replies, "'The Lord our God, the Lord is one; and you shall love the Lord your God with all your heart, and with all your soul, and with all your mind, and with all your strength.' The second is this, 'You shall love your neighbor as yourself.' There is no other commandment greater than these." In other words, even the Ten Commandments boil down to love. This is one of the most under-appreciated statements in the Bible. The assertion has immense implications for our understanding of the Ten Commandments and the usefulness of each of those commandments for ordering the Christian life.

Because Christ says there is one central concept, an unchanging character, threading its way through each of the ten seemingly different commandments, the implication is that they are more alike than they might appear. In the same way we can switch between ¼, 0.25, and 25% because they all mean the same thing, a person should be able to take any one of the Ten Commandments and, if it is properly understood, arrive at a restatement of the remaining nine commandments in terms of the one picked at the start. For instance, a person should be able to use the commandment "You shall not commit adultery" to imply that a person should also not lie, steal, worship false idols, and so on.

Pick adultery as a starting point, and this game is not that hard. Since every one of the commandments is about relationship and interrelationship, it is not much of a stretch to realize that committing adultery in the physical realm is similar to committing adultery in the spiritual realm by flirting with idols instead of remaining true to the one God of the first commandment. Nor is it so different from staying ethical (ethically pure) by not lying, cheating, and so on.

Thou Shalt Not Kill, Writ Large

Playing this game with other commandments is more challenging but also enlightening. One of my favorite starting points is the sixth commandment, "You shall not kill." No one thinks of themselves as a murderer, so this commandment is almost an afterthought for most people. But the moment a person notices that this commandment is not just about killing someone's body, the other nine commandments are necessary to clarify what else can be killed.

Not only should people refrain from murdering other people, the obvious meaning of the commandment, but neither should they kill their own spiritual walk with God by worshiping false idols or failing to rest on the Sabbath. In trying to win an argument, they should avoid killing the spirit or damaging the ego of another. Nor should they destroy another person's potential for love by callously using them for selfish, sexual ends before throwing them away. The longer the other commandments are considered in light of this one about murder, the more the commandments sound like descriptors of the wise, peacemaking love defined in 1 Corinthians. In meaning, they also begin to bear a remarkable resemblance to Martin Luther King, Jr.'s Six Principles of Nonviolence:

1. Nonviolence is a way of life for courageous people. It is active nonviolent resistance to evil.
2. Nonviolence seeks to win friendship and understanding. The end result of nonviolence is redemption and reconciliation.
3. Nonviolence seeks to defeat injustice, not people. Nonviolence recognizes that evildoers are also victims.

LOVE

4. Nonviolence holds that suffering can educate and transform. Nonviolence willingly accepts the consequences of its acts.

5. Nonviolence chooses love instead of hate. Nonviolence resists violence to the spirit as well as the body. Nonviolence love is active, not passive. Nonviolence love does not sink to the level of the hater. Love restores community and resists injustice. Nonviolence recognizes the fact that all life is interrelated.

6. Nonviolence believes that the universe is on the side of justice. The nonviolent resister has deep faith that justice will eventually win.[1]

All Our Parents

One of the most difficult commandments to start from in building toward the others is the fifth commandment, "Honor your father and your mother." Focus on the word honor, and meeting the challenge seems impossible. The key is to home in on our relationships with our fathers and mothers, not on the word honor as most people understand it. When I was a child and seriously crossed the line, my parents would remind me, "We brought you into this world, and we can usher you out." One can imagine God, Abba the Father, reminding us of the same thing if we decide to go chasing after other gods (first commandment). He might add that we will understand his anger when we have kids and grandkids of our own someday (second commandment).

Eventually, one begins to realize that the meaning of honor within this system of commandments is closer to the word "humility." In a global sense, the commandment asks us to have enough humility to remember that there is no such thing as pridefully imagining we pulled ourselves up by our own bootstraps. God and our parents brought us into this world; we would not be here without them. Enumerable public and Sunday school teachers functioning *in loco parentis* chose to share their time and talents to prepare us for adult life in this world. Every square mile of the

1. "Six Principles," paras. 1–6.

American ground we walk on was paid for by the blood of at least one soldier, not to mention forefathers and immigrant parents who risked everything for our futures. The fifth commandment is asking us to remember that we are fundamentally communal creatures paid for at significant cost. In light of that fact, it implores us to be humbler in loving honor of the sacrifices made on our behalf by so many hundreds and thousands, perhaps millions, of people, and certainly by our Father and one Lord.

Luther had something similar to say when he wrote about what it meant to be pious. "By piety," he began, "I mean that union of reverence and love to God which the knowledge of his benefits inspires. For until men feel that they owe everything to God, that they are cherished by his paternal care, and that he is the author of all their blessings . . . they will never submit to him in voluntary obedience."[2]

What Luther missed was, in the words of Christ, "that another commandment is like this": we should feel thankfulness and love for our neighbors and not just for God. Put another way, the quality of inward piety (reverence and love) for God is inextricably tied to the quality of our outward piety (respect and love) for our neighbors. All our neighbors. We cannot love God well without looking for and loving the good in our neighbors, parents included. And we cannot love our neighbors without first truly loving the goodness of God.

Little Gods and Big Consequences

Finally, it is useful to play this game with the second commandment, which for the longest time I thought was redundant in light of the first commandment. There is no easy way to rewrite any of the other commandments in a manner different than implied by the first commandment. That is, until a person realizes that what is unique about the second commandment is its close. This part finishes by saying, "For I the Lord your God am a jealous God,

---

2. Calvin, *Institutes of the Christian Religion*, 20.

visiting the iniquity of the father upon the children to the third and fourth generation of those who hate me, but showing steadfast love to thousands of those who love and keep my commandments."

Anyone who has participated in a ten-step program will recognize that this verse strongly suggests a worldview that sees sin and addiction as parallel processes. The consequences of addiction are never confined to just the addicted individual. They always spin out across family, friends, and future generations—tarnishing, jarring, damaging, and ruining lives in an ever-expanding infective circle. In this model, a surprising number of items can function as the *little gods* we worship when we seek relief from pain or an escape from feeling inadequate, fearful, depressed, or lonely.

The Serenity Bible used in many Alcoholics Anonymous programs includes the following in its list of possible addictive agents (little gods) that people can become dependent on as they seek unhealthy ways to escape the emotions they are feeling:

1. Alcohol or drugs
2. Work, achievement, and success
3. Money addictions, such as overspending, gambling, and hoarding
4. Control addictions, especially if they surface in personal, sexual, family, and business relationships
5. Food addictions
6. Sexual addictions
7. Approval dependency (the need to please people)
8. Rescuing patterns towards [sic] other persons
9. Dependency on toxic relationships (relationships that are damaging and hurtful)
10. Physical illness (hypochondria)
11. Exercise and physical conditioning
12. Cosmetics, clothes, cosmetic surgery, and trying to look good on the outside

13. Academic pursuits and excessive intellectualizing
14. Religiosity or religious legalism (preoccupation with the form and the rules and regulations of religion [with law and order], rather than benefiting from the real spiritual [wise-love] message)
15. General perfectionism
16. Cleaning and avoiding contamination and other obsessive-compulsive symptoms
17. Organizing and structuring (the need always to have everything in its place)
18. Materialism[3]

In reality, this list is a list of all the ways we try and wrest control from God's hands—control of our emotions, lives, and other people. These are the ways we try and place control in our own hands, despite his assertion that he is ultimately in control of everything. Whether we begin to lie, cheat, sleep around, or become violent in service to these controlling little gods, the real thrust of the second commandment is that we should be mindful of the consequences, not just to us but also to the many other people who are interdependent with us.

The point of all these different and more profound ways of understanding God's Ten Commandments is summarized in the Sermon on the Mount. There Christ said that he came to make the commandments whole. Then he began to expound on them in more depth than most Jews or Gentiles had ever considered. This depth came from one insight, a single underlying command that drove each and every one of the Ten Commandments: be more wisely and thoughtfully loving to God and humans, all humans, including our enemies and ourselves.

---

3. Hemfelt and Fowler, *Serenity*, 13–14.

What Is Lost When Grace Is Lost

THE ADMONISHMENT TO DO unto others as we do unto ourselves is both a command and an observation. Understanding this observation may be more important than the actual command itself. Suppose we desire to become loving people and to foster loving families and societies. In that case, Christ needs us to realize that it is impossible to love others wisely and well if we do not also love ourselves correctly.

There is a book called *The Zen of Tennis* by Dr. Joe Parent. The entire point of the book can be summed up in one sentence: "You are not your backhand." Neither people's backhands, nor their forehands, nor any other stroke they do or do not have in their arsenal defines who they are as people. If a coach says your backhand is terrible and you need to improve it, that assessment does not mean that you are personally also awful and need to work on remedying that situation.

Study a poor math student, and often you observe a student who at least halfway believes that being poor at algebra also means being inadequate as a person. Admire a super-achieving athlete or actress on top of the world, and more often than might be imagined you are looking at someone who is grappling with trauma or severe self-esteem issues. On a more mundane but ubiquitous level, most guys and more and more women these days are defined by their jobs. Work gives them their identity, their agency in the world, their self-esteem as patriarchal breadwinners filling their traditional roles or feminists "leaning in" to the demands of the times. Even if a person manages to escape these social sand traps, people who might never think of defining themselves by their golf strokes or baking skills still have no trouble filling the role of helicopter parents who define themselves by their children's performances.

Why should it be otherwise? That is exactly the wisdom of the world delivered by a society whose primary metric is the bottom line: The rich man is as good as his riches and the poor man as worthless as his empty wallet. It says that being a winner on the inside is inextricably tied to winning on the outside and that losers in the outside world are assuredly losers on the inside also.

Society is looking every which way as it tries to figure out why we and our children are ever more anxious, depressed, or addicted to this, that, or another agent. Could the diagnosis be as simple as observing that we live in a society that seems to run break-neck in the opposite direction of grace and redemptive kindness?

Will it make any difference how many consolation trophies we give out after childhood competitions if the broader society is intent on delivering the message that people *are* defined by where they finish in the race? We can try to insulate children from feeling more or less valued based on the outcome of the games they play or the grades they make. We can attempt to protect them from the harsh truth of an America where they really will be perceived as extensions of the jobs they hold, the money they earn, and the income and social connections their backhands win for them. But there should be no question at all about the destructive effects of living in a society that inextricably ties worth to achievement and worthlessness to a failure to achieve at satisfactory levels.

That is the subtle message delivered when parents look at people lower on the socio-economic ladder and say, without sufficient nuance, that such people are on the lower rungs because they deserve to be there. This is the message sent, express delivery, to impressionable young minds when we insist that poverty has no link to the time, place, or the family into which a person is born. That it has no connection to corporate greed and downsizing. That most people on the margins of society are there by their own failing, not because some aspects of hierarchy or existence perennially disenfranchise them from resources and possibilities more widely available to others.

It must be positively frightening for children trying to process such unforgiving, loveless, one-size-fits-all social beliefs about people who fail to *measure up*, who end up as white trash or black thugs, who cannot even claim the excuse of hurricanes, health emergencies, great depressions, recessions, or the factory closings that put them there. No, we say, they are there because they deserve to be there. And you will be too if you don't get your homework done because only winners' lives matter in the graceless and cruel society in which you are about to grow up.

First Corinthians says that our bodies are God's temples. Placing any other god but the God of grace on the central temple altar of who we are and how we judge worth destroys any real possibility of effectively exercising compassion and love for ourselves or others. At the very moment we most need those little gods to tell us that we are worthwhile and everything will be okay, they are gone. For it is when the gods of money, youth, security, and achievement have fled that we usually need them most.

More frightening for Christians who truly desire to exhibit peacemaking love, it is woefully hard to display compassion for another person when they arrive at our doorstep as a mirror image of what we, often unconsciously, are most fearful of one day reverting to or becoming. As human beings, our inner altars are and always will be blessed with God's grace, forgiveness, and enduring belief in our worth. His assessment is infinitely more generative than the one pro-offered by metrics based on our secular achievements or worldly possessions. Until we come to fully trust the reality of that truth for ourselves, it will remain difficult to see the same value in others who lack the trappings by which we more often judge worth.

There is understanding in remembering that tennis players are not their backhands. There is wisdom in bearing in mind that sinners are not their sins. It makes no difference how many inner altars and display cases each of us may be sporting; the only one that counts is the one upon which the God of love is present. The intrinsic worth his presence in each of us grants is a gift from God, not a product of our bootstraps and hands of which we can boast. That free gift is the foundation upon which humility, self-compassion, and the wise-love of God and other people are built.

Maturity through Grace and Love

FIGURE 12-1 IS A picture of the way a Christian comes to faith. Some people will think that the diagram of this process is backward. That is because believers in the faith-hope narrative tend to view faith as the beginning of the Christian journey. But faith is not the beginning of the Christian journey. Nor is it the end of that journey as it appears in this diagram. It is best understood as the middle.

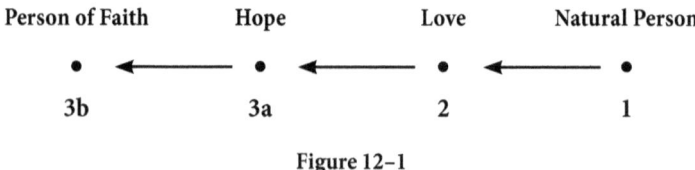

Figure 12-1

This is because the natural person does not simply arrive at the doorstep of faith and hope unbidden. The natural man cannot 1) save himself by pulling himself up by his spiritual bootstraps because he is not yet spiritual. Instead, he is 2) pursued by a loving God. He is surrounded by the gift of a created universe that continuously speaks to that love. He is helped by the love of teachers, friends, parents, neighbors, and even strangers who serve as God's hands, feet, and heart on earth. If people answer the constant knock, knock, knocking of this love, which began before they were even born, they awaken in time to 3a) hope in Christ and 3b) faith in God (see fig. 12-1).

Why do many faith-hope Christians believe that their choice to accept Christ's love is the beginning of the journey? Why do they trust that the second step on that journey opens access to the redemptive sacrifice of Christ and the hope of eternal life that results? The error arises because their understanding of that narrative tends to stop at Romans 8:33 with its emphasis on being the chosen, the special elect of God. This focus on the concept of election subtly introduces the idea of merit into the equation.

Contrast this with how grace (not merit) is the central fact of the trinitarian faith-hope-love worldview found throughout 1 Corinthians and in Romans if a person reads the entire book and not just the first part. There God's gracious love precedes both Christ's sacrifice and any hope a person has of coming to faith in him. By centering on love, the trinitarian narrative slams the door on merit, unavoidably throwing us, the wretched, onto the saving shores of amazing grace. It also reverses the direction of the story of coming to faith.

Why do we love God, the Scriptures ask? "We love, because he first loved us," 1 John 4:19 answers. God did not sacrifice his son because we deserved it. He did not do it because we merited it or because we were just that righteous. "God shows his love for us in that while we were yet sinners Christ died for us" (Rom. 5:8). No one comes to the Father except by the grace and love embodied in Christ's willing sacrifice. This grace, rooted in the undeserved nature of God's love toward us, is the sun around which all else orbits in the faith/hope/wise-love narrative.

Nope, No Turtles. It's Grace, Grace all the Way Down.

Being one of the chosen from an earthly point of view is great. Extrapolating on the positive notion of being communally chosen, many faith-hope Christians imagine an analogy wherein Americans are the new Israelites and America a new promised land delivered into our hands because we are exceptionally deserving. They overlook the part of the story where God told the chosen of old, "Know [sic] therefore, that the Lord your God is not giving you this good land to possess because of your righteousness; for you are a stubborn people" (Deut. 9:6). He then spends the remainder of the chapter reminding them how comically short they have fallen of any claim to merit.

Or take Romans where, after pointing the finger at the wickedness of the heathens, Paul turns back toward the Romans and says, "But you are many times worse." Same, too, in 1 Corinthians, where Paul writes, "It is actually reported that there is immorality among you, and of a kind that is not found even among pagans."

No matter how good we as Christians believe ourselves to be, no matter how great we imagine our church or nation to be, the truth is, "All have fallen short of the glory of God." Tempting as it is to argue the opposite, no person is good enough to get into heaven based on individual merit.

The inescapable, self-inflicted, and society-inflected nature of our sinfulness makes grace intrinsic to salvation, for no one needs saving who can save themself. Nor is this saving grace a one-time affair. Those who feel covered by grace do not say, "Yesterday we were undeserving, but now that we are saved, we are deserving." The mature Christian understands that we are daily saved anew. With each fresh prayer for forgiveness, we fall again upon God's grace. Like the athletes who constantly strive to improve, Christians should judge themselves by their worst rather than their best efforts. Instead, we tend to judge ourselves by our best efforts and others by their worst actions.

"Of course, it requires grace to get into heaven," many people will reply. But not without adding the caveat that, "On earth, I nonetheless merit all that I've earned by my cleverness and the sweat of my brow." Even when confronting this attitude, the Bible is firm on the point that all is grace. "Beware," Deuteronomy 8:17 begins. "Beware lest you say in your heart, 'My power and the might of my hand have gotten me this wealth.' You shall remember the Lord your God, for it is he who gives you power to get wealth; that he may confirm his covenant which he swore to your fathers, as at this day."

The centrality of grace to the Christian walk finds its greatest irony in the excuse many Christians cite for the way we treat many of our neighbors. The most popular reason given for not being kind, generous, or loving to this person or that group is, "They do not deserve it!" They do not deserve our tax dollars because they are not moral or hardworking. They do not deserve our help because they are not part of our tribe or team. They do not merit our love because they are not as human, as exceptional, as real, or as good as we are.

Are we being completely true to our faith when we—who must daily pray for grace—turn around and fail to offer grace and love to others as well? Are we people of integrity when we pray, "Forgive us our trespasses as we forgive those who trespass against us," and then believe that we can withhold the same forgiveness from others? Are we being honest with ourselves if we read, with no self-awareness, the parable of the servant whose king forgave him an immense debt? How is it possible to miss how similar we sometimes are to that same servant who was soon jailed for refusing to dismiss the lesser debt of someone else (Matt. 18:23–35)?

The grace God gives to us and the wise-love he asks us to give to others in return are one and the same. In God's eyes, is it not arrogant to believe otherwise—arrogant to think that we are deserving and others are less deserving, arrogant to assume that we are blameless and others mostly to blame for the brokenness in this fallen world? As fundamental as this truth is to a mature, biblical worldview, it is also the most challenging point of faith for many people to accept. This is because labeling others as undeserving or less deserving than we ourselves supposedly are is the primary way that many Christians skirt God's central commandment to do all they can, directly and indirectly, to love their neighbors.

We are commanded by grace to meet people where they are. We are beseeched by Christ to drop the first stones of indictment and disqualification. We are implored by love to find a way to value people and help them with their most pressing needs. Again, as a practical matter, what is the point of helping save someone who does not need saving? From a legal, economic, nationalistic, or tribal perspective, the prisoner, the poor, the immigrant, the outcast can all be classed as undeserving. Yet it is precisely their lack of worldly merit that makes them most in need of grace so that they, like us, can enjoy God's redemptive love, both temporally and spiritually.

Christian Maturity: Coming Full-circle in Love

Figure 12-1 presents the process of coming to faith as a line. Though useful for discussion, this gives a distorted view of how a believer is supposed to grow to maturity because it posits love as the beginning of the story and faith as the end. In reality, God's wise-love is both the alpha (A) and the omega (Ω) of the Christian walk. As figure 12-2 illustrates, the love given to us by God and others opens a doorway to hope and Christian faith. But maturing in our faith takes practice. Until we begin returning to God and other people the love we received first, we will remain as children. Maturity is found in actions that speak louder than clanging words, not in hypocritical talk lacking in the fruit of actionable, human love.

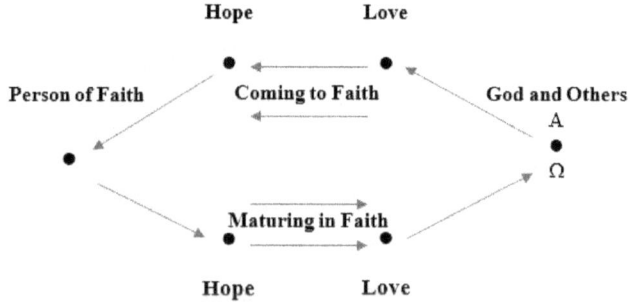

Figure 12-2

The way God and others have first loved us (the top arc of arrows in fig. 12-2) provides the template by which we are supposed to love others (the bottom arc of arrows in fig. 12-2). Faith marks the beginning of that new walk, the first baby steps into a new life. Loving with an increasingly wise heart points the way to the ultimate end of that walk and to maturity in Christ and society.

Maturity through Grace and Love

Step one in this process is learning humility. Some Christians take a pejorative approach to helping people. They make them feel small, like children only they can save. On the other hand, mature Christians should be more like the mountains, the sky, or God himself in their paradoxical ability to make people feel small but not inadequate, tiny but part of something grand and enlarging.[1] True humility simultaneously makes paupers and princes of both the bearer and recipient. It allows God and others to be so mysterious that we feel drawn to understand their perspective and respect their unknown potential. Thus, humility is the gateway to spiritual maturity and wise-love.

Like breathing in is to breathing out,[2] this makes cultivating a reflexive ability to be gracious to other people the next step in exercising wise-love. Unaware of the various assumptions we bring to bear when dealing with people, we may want to believe we have sufficient understanding to judge their situations. But we are not Christ standing at the well with full knowledge of the social outcast before him. We generally know next to nothing about the person across town or even in front of us.

Unlike Christ, we cannot move forward in love until we are willing to listen, observe, value, and empathize. If we have not listened closely enough to repeat to the other person or group how many children they have, their spouses' names, what tragedies they may have endured, what dreams, hopes, and fears they possess, how biblically gracious is that? A rather scary thought is that some of us may not even know the true story of some items on that list, even with our family members.

And of course, from beginning to end, we need to embrace patience and the genuine loss of control represented by submitting to God's timing. Our job as Christians is to tirelessly sow the seeds of generosity, kindness, and compassion. Where those seeds land and how long they take to grow, if they grow at all, is not up to us. Love may fall on a parched soul or take only shallow root. But in

---

1. Fynn, *Mister God*, 105–106.
2. Talbot, "Week One Chaplain Tewell," para. 9.

ways and places that are woefully hard to predict, grace can make any seed flourish. Whatever the course, our job is to love patiently.

This perspective on how the faith of each Christian comes to maturity by growing in love shifts the nature of evangelism from an activity someone intentionally decides to do to something that eventually emanates, without choice or even words, from the very heart of a new life increasingly vested in love. The pear tree does not think to itself, "It is now time to bud and bear fruit." For a real pear tree, bearing pears is something that proceeds without choice (and in concert with God's timing) from the innermost nature of what it means to be a pear tree. So, too, for Christians, for whom the type and abundance of fruit is a sign of the quality of faith.

Several times in Proverbs, the writer begins passages with the phrase, "Three things I know are alike," and then he presents his list of pairs. I want to add another pair to the list: I have seen maidens and men so attractive that everyone with eyes turns to look when they walk into a room. I have also seen souls so magnificent that people cannot help but aspire to the gracious faith they display.

The Secular Versus the Sacred

So, what is the difference between souls that belong to the dust versus those that belong to the divine—and why such different destinies? This question would seem to be about what is secular and what is sacred. But the character difference between the two is best understood in terms of their relationship to time. Worldly/secular concerns tend to be more short-term in nature. This is why we also refer to them as temporal concerns. Eternal concerns are, obviously, longer in term. This temporal/eternal dichotomy is enlightening when comparing the course of the faith-hope narrative to that of the faith-hope-love narrative.

Many two-step Christians see nothing wrong with the pitch offered by the faith-hope promise. If the person says, "Yes!", for many people who prefer this narrative, that is the end of the story: Got faith? Check. Guaranteed to make it to heaven? Check and done!—Very individual. Very private. Two short steps. And ever in danger of falling back into the low gravity of secular concerns for failing to aspire to a higher orbit.

Compare that to the three-step, faith-hope-love journey. It takes patience to build a long-term personal relationship with Christ while embracing the faith he offers. But in doing so, a person is asked to ascend the foothills and ever-higher false peaks of aspiring to mature love. That is a lengthier proposition.

When Christ offers this free gift of grace, it is not actually scot-free. It cost us something to accept. We must spend time and effort opening our minds and hearts to receive his gift of forgiveness and love. But on the faith-hope-love path, this is doubly true because we must then open them again to give that gift away to others. Only then is the eternal circle of divine love complete.

Or consider the different prosperity gospels embodied in each of these worldviews. The good news of faith-hope is strongly biased toward an earthly gospel of prosperity. It favors the idea that keeping the faith and giving first fruits to God results in merit, increased status, success, and earthly wealth. The faith-hope-love narrative also has its version of the prosperity gospel. But it is a longer-term version. By loving graciously and expansively over the long years of our lives, Christians build up "treasures in heaven where moths and rust do not consume."

Because humans tend toward selfishness, any version of the Good News that fails to emphasize a) how love allows us to begin the journey of faith and b) the need for love's maturing influence on the road to completing that journey will almost always pull us in a secular direction. It will gravitate toward individual concerns and away from communal sacrifices. It will move toward a comfortable certainty and away from a discomforting embrace of eternal mystery—toward short-term ends and away from that which is sustainable and never-ending.

What will our coworkers say this afternoon if we look weak by turning the other cheek in the morning meeting? What will the neighbors think tomorrow if we are kind to the wrong people today? What might happen to my job a few weeks from now if I fail to look out for myself, my family, and my country first and foremost? These are secular questions that will fade with the grass. By contrast, wise-love—in seeking a balanced way to pay forward the grace we have received—plants its flag squarely in the golden soil of eternity. Therein lies the truly Good News of the gospel: that by accepting the open invitation to go forth in faith, hope, and love, we can set foot on a road that will never end.

Evidence of the Protective Wisdom Love Provides

THIS BOOK BEGAN WITH the assertion that wise-loving people can act in the beforehand of partial knowledge as they would have acted in the hindsight of complete understanding. At every stage of life, we encounter choices that lead down one path or another. With every news cycle, we hear would-be prophets saying we should pick this candidate or that one if the nation is to be saved. The certainty wise-love provides in making the right decision in these situations was advanced, but evidence of its actual effectiveness has been mentioned only in bits and pieces up to this point. So before closing, this final point needs to be addressed directly.

Because many decisions we are currently making have not yet played out, we will end the way we began: by looking backward in time, starting with slavery and the Civil War. On the eve of the war between the blue and grey, what if (unknowing of the outcome) we had used the tenets of wise-love to gauge which side would be more likely to win and so which cause to join? Both sides believed in God. But based on what each side said in their constitutions, the South had a very different conception of the type of love favored by God as compared to the Northern conception.

The North's Constitution (the original American Constitution) favored "the common good." The South's banished that term. The Northern Constitution allowed states to choose if they wished to become slave states or remain free states. The Southern Constitution "insisted on its own way," making it mandatory that all states embrace slave statutes if the South won the war. The North was patient; the South was not. It just had to be the one to fire the first shot. And so on. The final result? The North, which sided more with the tenets of wise-love, won.

One could attribute the victory to luck. But a person could also look at the North's leader, Lincoln. As testified to by the perennial bouts of depression, political defeat, and personal tragedy he suffered on his road to serving the greater good, Lincoln was an imperfect man who "bore all things, believed all things, endured all things" for the love of country and the human ideals for which it stood. He did not "insist on his own way" but put his political enemies into key positions, listened to what they had to say, and often took their advice. Borrowing a quote from the online Encyclopedia Britannica about Lincoln's character, "In the midst of the Civil War, . . . the *Washington Chronicle* found a resemblance between him and George Washington in their 'sure judgment, perfect balance of thoroughly sound faculties, and great calmness of temper, great firmness of purpose, supreme moral principle, and intense patriotism.'"[1] The *Buffalo Express* referred to his "remarkable moderation and freedom from passionate bitterness."[2]

Or take another historical character, Truman, whom half of America worried would fail the presidential test of time. One reason many people were so concerned was that he lacked a college degree. His educational shortcomings ended up being of little consequence. The decisions he made were in close accord with wise-love, allowing both post-war America and the world to prosper. When he could have set America up as an atomic-bomb-wielding king and most defeated nations as vessels, instead he chose the Marshall Plan to feed both his friends and enemies alike and to help all rebuild. It was an astonishing act of kindness, the complete opposite of the Treaty of Versailles that made the WWI German losers bow and grovel so low that Hitler eventually rose to power, with WWII soon following in his wake.

---

1. Current, "Abraham Lincoln," para. 4.
2. Current, "Abraham Lincoln," para. 4.

Evidence of the Protective Wisdom Love Provides

Though we could pick many other examples to illustrate the leaders people should favor in the absence of complete information, one example from antiquity offers a fitting conclusion: Cyrus II, whose Persian empire eventually spanned most of the known world. The Scriptures refer to him as "the anointed one" when speaking of his role in freeing the Jews from their Babylonian captivity and returning the temple to Jerusalem. How would a Jew of that day have known whether or not to believe God's prophecies of a leader so decidedly outside the Jewish tribal tradition? Not that they had much choice in the matter, but if they had been able to vote, was there anything about Cyrus's character that would have recommended they hang their hat on him?

Here are a few descriptions of Cyrus. As Cassandane, Cyrus's first wife, lay dying, she said that she found it more bitter to leave Cyrus than to depart her life.[3] Surprisingly for a world conqueror, Cyrus did not "insist on his own way" but "respected the customs and religions of conquered lands."[4] Xenophon, the great Greek historian, wrote of him in his *Cyropaedia*, saying, "And those who were subject to him, he treated with esteem and regard, as if they were his own children, while his subjects themselves respected Cyrus as their 'Father.' . . . What other man but 'Cyrus,' after having overturned an empire, ever died with the title of 'the Father' from the people whom he had brought under his powers? For it is plain fact that this is a name for one that bestows, rather than one that takes away!"[5] Cyrus represents the epitome of one who ruled with wise-love rather than in the name of greed, aggrandizing power, or hate.

The success of all these men, despite their human failings, hinged on the wise inclusion of the very people they could have most easily disenfranchised. For Lincoln, success came not only because he included his political enemies in decision-making but also because he finally decided to emancipate the 3.5 million slaves that comprised almost 40 percent of the Southern population.

---

3. Kohl, *The Earthly Republic*, 198.
4. Dandamayev, "Cyrus II," para. 20.
5. Watson and Dale, *The Cyropaedia*, 272.

That is 40 percent of the people that, had they been conscripted for the South rather than viewed as cowardly and unfit for battle, could easily have tipped the scales in favor of a quick Confederate victory. For Truman, the ensuing worldwide prosperity of his Pax Americana resulted in equally unparalleled prosperity at home. It was almost as if he were following the Cyrus template.

Yet none of this should be surprising. Research shows that doing unto all others as we would have them do unto us—listening to them, considering their needs, including them—really does have surprisingly positive returns. Multiple studies have shown that helping others increases one's own happiness and longevity. But a recent study discovered that "volunteerism lengthened lives only when the volunteerism was done for selfless reasons." Helping those who can help you is not as beneficial as helping those who cannot help you, those outside your regular social class, generation, or other identity groups.[6] Other studies have shown that the most significant predictor of the happiness and well-being of a country's native population is the happiness of their non-native populations. If immigrants of all kinds are happy and healthy, the same will be true for the native population.[7] Even simply meditating on how we can help others shows surprising benefits.[8]

The point made here is that when we find ourselves in the voting booth, unsure of which button to push for lack of sufficient information, we could do a lot worse than simply asking which candidate and what percentage of their followers display the characteristics of wise-love: tending not to insist on their way alone, being patient and kind rather than rude or resentful, showing a verifiable willingness to sacrifice on behalf of others, displaying confidence without being arrogant. Although no candidate will be perfect, the one closest to this description will always bring the better outcome. Even more than tribal allegiance, a willingness to try and make peace on behalf of all tribes, at least those tribes

---

6. Seppälä, "Overlooked Secret to Longevity," para. 5.
7. Astor, "Want to Be Happy?" para. 11.
8. Seppälä, "Overlooked Secret to Longevity," para. 6.

Evidence of the Protective Wisdom Love Provides

willing to make peace, is a crucial component of a wise-loving leadership style.

As for life decisions unrelated to picking leaders, wise-love is still the most accurate marker on the road to the best possible life a person can live. Unable to decide between one job or career and another? Ask which one will allow you to help more people, which path will pull you closer or further away from growing into a wise-loving person. If you still wish to go with a career that seems less suited to a wise-love approach, ask if you can modify the job in a way that will allow you to be true to the tenets of wise-love. Are there volunteer or pro bono opportunities that will enable you to exercise wise-love regularly?

Are you looking for someone with whom you can spend the rest of your life? Ask if the person you are considering is patient, kind, humble, hopeful, and resilient. Does your perspective spouse tend toward bitterness and resentment or toward level-headedness? More importantly, do those traits also describe you, or are you both at least complementary on these wise-love traits? Finally, because one of these traits seems more important than the others when it comes to marriage, I have to especially agree with a piece of advice that I once received: Marry someone who is not wedded to insisting on his or her own way, someone who is flexible. That wise-love trait makes a tremendous difference in the quality of a marriage, especially if it is characteristic of both partners.

But do not take my word for these things. Pick people across the historical, social, and religious spectrum, ask to what degree their character displays the tenets of wise-love, and then look at the positive or negative difference in outcomes that resulted. In the short term, people who measure lower on the wise-love scale often have better success. But for long-term, sustainable success, the people, organizations, and nations that hitch their wagons to the tenets of wise-love more often than not end up being the real winners.

Wise-Love Reprised

IF I HAD TO capture the way of wise-love in a nutshell, I would hinge the summary on a rephrasing of the ethic by which Colonel Steven dePyssler lived every day of his 101 years on earth. After logging thirty-nine years in the military (becoming one of the few United States soldiers to have served in World War II, the Korean War, the French Indochina War, and the Vietnam War), he went on to spend his days helping fellow veterans for an additional forty-one years. In 2019, dePyssler was still working. Shortly thereafter, he contracted the Coronavirus and died.[1] Before his passing, he was quoted as saying he had aimed to help one person, every day, for as long as he lived.[2]

On the surface, dePyssler reminds me of many salt-of-the-earth Christians I know. They are good people who daily seek to do all the good they can do for family and friends. They do this in solid accordance with the demands of faith and hope. Yet, according to 1 Corinthians and many other portions of the Bible, caring only for family and friends is insufficient. Nor did Colonel dePyssler live his life as if he believed such a limited effort at love was enough. To rephrase the motto I saw alive in dePyssler, and to give the most concise statement of the love 1 Corinthians is asking of us, "As Christians, all of us should strive to help at least one person inside our tribes and one person outside our tribes, every day, for as long as we live."

1. Sedacca, "Col. dePyssler, Aided Veterans' Families," paras. 1, 9.
2. Ferrell, "Col. dePyssler, Unofficial Mayor," para. 13.

Some people will object. They will say that they do not live close enough to anyone who is not family, friend, or of the same tribe to make meeting this obligation easy. But that is the point, as well as a neatly packaged proof of the importance of the issue. Many people complain about immigrants and outsiders living in Little Mexicos, Chinatowns, and dilapidated black neighborhoods. They gripe about these residents' failure to acculturate. But such segregation exists partly because many Christian Americans are so busy living out the American dream in gated communities and rural/suburban-faith enclaves that they forget to open the door and invite in anyone else. And that is stating the problem in the politest way possible.

The moment I saw dePyssler in action, it was easy to see how far short our family was from putting his version of intra- and extra-tribal love into practice. With him in mind, the first round of questions at our family dinner table each evening has begun to include asking what we have each done to help at least one person inside our tribe and outside our tribe that day. Early on in attempting this change of habit, we found that it was far too easy to arrive at evening meal with nothing to tell. We quickly learned that having conversations at breakfast, on the way to school, or occasionally at lunch about how we were planning to be helpful made our efforts more intentional and more likely to succeed by dinner. What if every Christian in the country began attempting to love one person inside their tribe and one person outside their tribe in the same practical, everyday fashion as dePyssler?

Socio-Religious Narcissism

For a while, I tried to live out his ethic in light of Matthew 25:40: "As you did it to one of the least of these my brethren, you did it to me." But people, including myself, can be so trying that I quickly gave up. A more workable approach hinged on remembering Genesis 1:27. The verse says that God created each of us in his image. It implies we all have something of Christ inside—not the fullness of Christ, but something of what made him special. Genesis 1:27

provides the basis for understanding that we are obliged to seek what is unique and deserving of love in everyone. Instead of disappointedly giving up when we encounter imperfections, we can expect them while also remembering the admonition to search deeper for the good that is God-ordained to be there.

I hear people dismiss the other side in too many discussions—out of hubris or self-righteousness—before they have tried to look deeper. It is as if they feel that acknowledging the validity of another person—the truth of one point, one desire, one hope by someone in another tribe—is an arch betrayal of their own social, religious, intellectual, or political clan. That mindset robs us of one of the most important avenues we have for the daily exercise of loving others: listening intently enough to find some common ground. How would life change if, spurred on by the wise-love ethic, we began stepping sufficiently outside of our communal bounds to make listening to such alternative views a regular and welcome possibility?

Or consider a practical application of what 1 Corinthians says about how love should avoid jealousy and boastfulness. When was the last time—while scrolling through our Instagram or Facebook feeds—we admitted that those infinite threads of perfectly curated lives sometimes made us jealous of other people, especially of extra-tribal competitors who seemed like they might be surpassing us?[3] When did we last acknowledge in a reply that there are more ways of looking at the world than just our way? When is the last memory we have of embracing a humble, peacemaking co-narrative of events rather than an arrogant "we know better than you" alternative-narrative of events?

In short, when did we last steer our months, weeks, and days away from a mode of life that increasingly resembles a kind of social and religious narcissism—replete with paranoia, fear, and an inability to accept anyone else's viewpoint as valid or to place anyone else's interest above our own individual, family, national, or tribal self-interests? Peacemaking compromise is not a bad thing if it is done honestly and allows both sides a reasonable measure

---

3. Pointed out by Heather K., 2020.

of self-respect and acknowledged worth. But compromise and the acceptance of multiple cooperating narratives is not something that social or religious narcissism has ever taken lying down.

For a front-row seat to what such social narcissism looks like when codified, it is helpful to compare the Constitution of the Confederacy to the U.S. Constitution. The two documents differ by a little over 900 words. Those differences are both by inclusion and exclusion, with 84 percent of the Confederate version being an exact copy of the American version. From the outset, the Confederate version is clear on its social goals. Unlike the United States Constitution, the Confederate preamble makes sure to include that it is God-ordained. Then, ironically, it immediately eliminates any mandate to use its God-ordained freedoms for the common good.

Gone were the phrases that emphasized the American need to "provide for the common defense [sic]" or "promote the general welfare." Gone was the aspiration toward a mystical "union." Banished were the notion of humility and the need for change and growth. Confederate authors replaced these ideas with a philosophy of permanent, individualistic self-interest, "each State [and by extension each individual] acting in its sovereign and independent character."

The difference between these two documents highlights the central social, political, and religious tension of our times, indeed of the entire history of the United States: What are we supposed to do with the blessings and freedom God has given us? Are we supposed to use them for the common good of all American tribes or for the individual comfort of a single tribe? Are we supposed to celebrate that an 1860s, seven-percent, plantation-lord ruling class once acquired 75 percent of a society's wealth (similar to the 2020, one-percent business elite)?[4] Are we supposed to reserve civil rights for only one tribe while failing to help—with our actions, votes, and prayers—extend those rights and opportunities to all people, even those we are sure do not deserve our help? These are the 1 Corinthians questions Paul is asking and answering when

---

4. Du Bois, *Black Reconstruction in America*, pg. 32.

he tells us that, at least for Christians, personal freedom should be exercised in service to expansive, courageous, peacemaking love.

The Practicalities of Compromise

As a footnote to the need for such love, it is essential to remember that the Pilgrims did not come to America because they were fleeing persecution. They came because they did not know how to follow 1 Corinthians's command to be in the world but not of the world. On the final leg of their journey, they were fleeing from a Dutch homeland that accepted everybody's way of doing things.

In a land practiced in making peace with everyone, the Pilgrims hated not being able to insist that their religious way was the only right way. So, they journeyed to America, where the abundant space allowed them to live in isolated communities. There they used their newfound freedom to ensure that converts and practitioners were, ironically, not nearly as open-minded or free as the broader country permitted.

This story illustrates the huge contradiction resting at the center of the belief that America is one nation under God. The paradox is that many Christians who are quickest to make that claim are just as quick in jettisoning the central 1 Corinthians truth that freedom and consensus are best nurtured with humility and love. They insist on their own way with seemingly no sense that there is more than one way to skin a spiritual cat in many cases. Among the least preached upon verses in their circles are 1 Corinthians 8:2, which says, "If anyone imagines he knows something [with certainty], he does not yet know as he ought to know"; 1 Corinthians 10:23, which asserts, "All things are lawful, but not all things are helpful. All things are lawful but not all things build up"; and 1 Corinthians 5:12, which admonishes us not to judge non-Christians but to judge ourselves first and to throw out those who profess to be *our type of Christian* but who flout the very standards by which they insist others live.

What would a debate on abortion look like among Christian denominations if every statement were honestly preceded by phrases like, "I know I see only in a mirror dimly, so maybe you have a part of the truth, too," or, "As certain as I would like to be, I know that there are limits to my understanding, so tell me what you see that I may be missing," or, "You know, I don't fully agree with you, but if all things are lawful, if there is truly a season for every matter under heaven, then perhaps I should listen to you long enough to find something useful in what you have to say?"

People who are used to moving about the world in love understand the concept of a wise middle ground. It is where each person takes what he knows and combines it with what others know to come up with an understanding that is better than any of them could have arrived at if left to their own lonely and loveless devices. As the young lead character in the book *Mr. God, this is Anna* likes to say, people have individual points of view, but God has an infinite number of viewing points. The more we combine our individual points of view into co-narrative solutions as opposed to competing narrative perspectives, the closer we come to something approaching God's infinite number of viewing points and his wisdom.

When people repeatedly refuse to do others the daily kindness of accepting practical middles, it is both an abdication of peacemaking love and an admission of a hidden agenda. That agenda often includes selfishness, exclusion, hate, or an unhealthy interest in controlling others more than ourselves. On this last point, when 1 Corinthians 5:12 inquires, "For what have I to do with judging outsiders? Is it not those inside the church whom you are to judge?", Paul is highlighting a very Christian temptation. We want to ask extra-tribal members to live up to standards we as a group do not live up to ourselves. This sinful tendency explains why, during anti-abortion battles, it is conveniently forgotten that Christians undergo the lion's share, 54 percent, of the very abortions we are trying to curtail.[5] It explains why men tend to be the ones pushing the harshest abortion laws while conveniently forgetting to include themselves in the legal consequences.

---

5. Jones, "People of All Religions Have Abortions," paras. 13–15.

Love

Immigration, homelessness, and any number of problems become insoluble the moment the dominant tribe imposes more of the blame and so more of the work onto the shoulders of those it wishes to keep subordinate or push outside. The refusal to make peace, to call ourselves to at least half account in almost any community problem, is the opposite of wise-love. It is an invitation to communal ruin because God does indeed answer prayers, never forgetting to forgive us of our sins, but only as long as we do not forget to forgive and reinvest in others as well.

A natural trinity resides inside any healthy house. The paternal, Old Testament, law-and-order, tribal viewpoint is ever mindful that the unyielding demands of God the Father are always present. The maternal, New Testament, mercy-and-grace viewpoint that embraces the demands of Christ the Son is also resident. But in keeping with dePyssler's daily kindness, this trinity is not complete unless the wise, peacemaking love of the Spirit is included. It must be alive in any house that wishes to stand undivided against itself. How do the rigid demands of law and order find a balance with Christ's call for mercy and grace if not through love? Amid the constant, ever-shifting sea of growth and change, love bears all things, believes all things, hopes all things, and endures all things. Love is the strong tie that binds. Without the wisdom of love, we as a nation, as communities, and as families will amount to nothing but the passing of the wind.

Bibliography

Astor, Maggie. "Want to Be Happy? Try Moving to Finland." https://www.nytimes.com/2018/03/14/world/europe/worlds-happiest-countries.html.
Banks, Adelle M. "The Bible—helpful, but not read much." https://religionnews.com/2017/04/25/the-bible-helpful-but-unread/.
Berding, Kenneth. "Something About the Book of Romans that will Help You Really 'Get' It." https://www.biola.edu/blogs/good-book-blog/2012/something-about-the-book-of-romans-that-will-help-you-really-get-it.
Calvin, John. *Institutes of the Christian Religion, Kindle Edition*. Overland Park, KS: Digireads.com, 2017.
"Corinth." abrock.com. https://www.abrock.com/Greece-Turkey/corinth.html.
Current, Richard N. "Abraham Lincoln." *Encyclopedia Britannica*. https://www.britannica.com/biography/Abraham-Lincoln/Reputation-and-character.
Dandamayev, Muhammad A. "Cyrus III. Cyrus II The Great." *Encyclopaedia Iranica*. https://iranicaonline.org/articles/cyrus-iiI.
"Drum Major Instinct." The Martin Luther King, Jr. Research and Education Institute. https://kinginstitute.stanford.edu/encyclopedia/drum-major-instinct.
Du Bois, W. E. B. *Black Reconstruction in America: 1860–1880*. New York: Touchstone, 1995.
Ferrell, Scott. "Col. Steven L. dePyssler, unofficial 'Mayor of Barksdale Air Force Base,' dies at 101." https://www.shreveporttimes.com/story/news/local/2020/07/25/retired-col-steven-depyssler-dies-101-barksdale-air-force-base/5511743002/.
Fynn. *Mister God, This Is Anna*. New York City: Ballantine, 1974.
Hemfelt, Dr. Robert, and Dr. Richard Fowler. *Serenity: A Companion for Twelve Step Recovery, Complete with New Testament, Psalms & Proverbs*. Nashville: Thomas Nelson, 1990.
Jones, Rachel K. "People of All Religions Use BirthControl." https://www.guttmacher.org/article/2020/10/people-all-religions-use-birth-control-and-have-abortions.
Kohl, Benjamine G., et al. *The Earthly Republic: Italian Humanists on Government and Society*. Philadelphia, PA: University of Pennsylvania,

Bibliography

1978. https://books.google.com/books?id=EQfpAAAAIAAJ&q=Cyrus%27s+love+for+Cassandane&pg=PA198#v=snippet&q=Cyrus's%20love%20for%20Cassandane&f=false.

"Martin Luther 95 Theses." Uncommon Travel, Germany. https://www.uncommon-travel-germany.com/martin-luther-95-theses.html#martinluther95theses21.

O'Neal, Sam. "Earliest Days of the Roman Christian Church." https://www.learnreligions.com/the-early-church-at-rome-363409.

Parry, Reginals St. John, ed. *The First Epistle of Paul the Apostle to the Corinthians.* London: Cambridge University Press, 1957. https://archive.org/details/firstepistleofpaoooounse/page/n11/mode/1up.

Sedacca, Matthew. "Col. Steven dePyssler, Who Aided Veterans' Families, Dies at 101." https://www.nytimes.com/2020/08/09/obituaries/col-steven-depyssler-dead-coronavirus.html.

Seppälä, Ph.D. Emma. "The Greatest and Most Overlooked Secret to Longevity." https://www.psychologytoday.com/us/blog/feeling-it/201304/the-greatest-and-most-overlooked-secret-longevity.

"SIX PRINCIPLES OF NONVIOLENCE." The Martin Luther King, Jr. Center for Nonviolent Social Change. https://kinginstitute.stanford.edu/sites/mlk/files/lesson-activities/six_principles_of_nonviolence.pdf.

Smith, John. *Book of Knowledge.* London: Cambridge University Press, 1990.

Talbot, Mary Lee. "WATCH: Week One chaplain Tewell reflects on life of faith at Sunday Vespers." https://chqdaily.wordpress.com/2013/06/24/watch-rev-thomas-k-tewell/.

Watson, John Selby, and Henry Dale, trans. *The Cyropaedia, or, Institution of Cyrus, and the Hellenics, or Grecian history. Literally translated from the Greek of Xenophon.* London: H.G. Bohn, 1855. https://archive.org/details/cyropaediaorinsooxeno/page/272/mode/2up.

Woodard, Colin. *American Nations: A History of the Eleven Rival Regional Cultures of North America.* New York City: Penguin, 2012.

www.ingramcontent.com/pod-product-compliance
Lightning Source LLC
Chambersburg PA
CBHW070321100426
42743CB00011B/2506